PROFESSIONAL WRESTLING IN MISSISSIPPI

········ A HISTORY ········

JEFFREY MARTIN

FOREWORD BY GIL CULKIN

THE
History
PRESS

Published by The History Press
Charleston, SC
www.historypress.com

Front cover, left to right: Tonya Rowland; Star Shots by Christy, owner, Christy Harville; Gil Culkin.
Back cover, top, left to right: Wikimedia Commons; Library of Congress; Tia Howell; Wikimedia Commons; *bottom*: Star Shots by Christy, owner, Christy Harville.

First published 2023

ISBN 9781540257185

Library of Congress Control Number: 2022951585

CONTENTS

CONTENTS

FOREWORD

When Jeffrey Martin first contacted me and told me about the book he was working on about the history of professional wrestling in the state of Mississippi, I had no idea of the depth and detail he would be going into and the untold amount of time he has obviously spent doing research. Having written a book myself on my personal experience promoting during the 1970s–80s, I can assure you it is quite an undertaking. I focused mainly on that particular period. Jeffrey has gone way beyond that, doing a deep dive into the history from the very beginning to beyond my time as a promoter. When he sent me a copy of his manuscript, I found that the details, names, times and places he was able to come up with truly amazing. When he asked me my thoughts on it and whether I would consider writing a foreword for his book, it was without hesitation that I said, "Yes, I will be happy to."

Having grown up in a wrestling family, I was fairly familiar with a great deal of the history of professional wrestling in Mississippi, mostly through my father's many articles and pictures from his days in the sport starting in the late 1930s and the many stories he told me, then through my own involvement with him on the promotional end of it. However, what Jeffrey has managed to put together has taught this old dog an awful lot and has filled in a lot of blanks for me. He takes you on a journey in such a way that you just have to keep reading. His passion and dedication to this project are clear.

Wrestling throughout the years has always been a huge form of excitement and entertainment for so many families in the South. It holds so many memories for so many people. Pretty much any wrestler who was a big name at the time, or who later became a big name, came through Mississippi. Many actually got their start here. When I decided to write my book, it was not intended to be about myself but to document a certain period, because so many people had reached out to me many years later with questions and interest about those days. There is something to be said for Jeffrey, who has such a passion to learn about and document the history of professional wrestling in Mississippi. This book is not about him. It is about the men and women—the legends—who paved the way for the stars of today.

It still amazes me that so many people want to know more, whether they are old enough to remember or are just now becoming fans of wrestling and want to learn more about its origin and history in Mississippi. It is an amazing journey through the years. It is very important to preserve and document this history. Jeffrey has done an amazing job in doing so. The wrestling of years past can never be brought back, but they can and should be remembered and passed on for future generations to read.

Having grown up in the wrestling business and being fortunate to be a part of it for a time, I realize that it was just a small part of the territory days. I was a young man in the right place at the right time. I wouldn't give up the experience and memories for anything, but I realize there is a much bigger story to be told. It is an amazing story. Whether you are a wrestling buff, a history buff in general or even a young wrestler today, this book is a must read. When you read about the wrestlers and promoters from the early days, you will find yourself picturing them in your mind. I know I did. This book is a great contribution to the wrestling community. Thank you, Jeffrey, for asking me to write this. It is my pleasure, and I highly recommend your book. Job very well done.

—Gil Culkin

ACKNOWLEDGEMENTS

First, I must thank my lord and savior, Jesus Christ, for the gift of life and for giving me the ability to see this project through. Also, I want to thank my family for the sacrifices they made to allow me the time to write this book. This includes my wife, my sons and a host of other wonderful and supportive family members. I want to thank all those who took the time to discuss their experiences in this fascinating business with me and those who allowed me to use their wonderful photographs for the book. This list includes Kenny Valiant, Gil Culkin, John Horton, Dennis Upton, Lolly Griffin, David Haskins, Jimmy Blaylock, Randy Hales, Kathy Hinds Moore, Rodney Grimes, Aaron Holt, Billy McClain, Marcus Dupree, Christy Harville, Rex Luther, Edith Poole, Tony Dabbs, Joel Gillentine, Carol Springfield Carman, Tonya Rowland, Josh and Kristen Newell, Doug McKay, Sheryl Ewing, Steve Starr, "Gun Show" Brett Michaels and Buddy Huggins.

Thanks goes to Shane Palmer-Pinnell, for providing information on his stepfather, Max Palmer. To Adam Armour, Blake Alsup and everyone at Journal Inc., thank you for all your help throughout the process. Kristina Stancil and Mark Neaves, thanks for inspiring me to start writing with purpose. Thanks to Maria Everett for providing me with information on the Tupelo American Legion. Lastly, I would like to thank everyone who has encouraged me throughout the process.

INTRODUCTION

I must confess! When I began writing this book, I thought it would be easy. How complex could the history of professional wrestling be? I quickly realized how wrong I was. I realized there were limitations in the breadth of information I could include in a single book on this topic. The origin of the sport and its rise to popularity are multilayered and complex, and the stories told in the ring and those that happened outside the ring each deserve documentation. I hope to release several works later to help contextualize the information in this book.

When I began filling in the blanks in my knowledge of professional wrestling, more blanks appeared. I learned to consider each as its own little mystery and to find enjoyment as I resolved those mysteries. Sadly, I also had to come to terms with the idea that not all mysteries can be solved. I still pursue these, but I do not let their uncertainty keep me from telling as much of the story as possible.

In this book, I outline the major events and promotions in the history of professional wrestling in Mississippi. I discuss everything from the bare-knuckle boxing matches that nearly killed wrestling in its infancy to today's "outlaw" promotions, where weekday laborers spend a few hours each weekend becoming the hero or villain they have envisioned since they were children. Some do this in the hope of someday achieving fame in wrestling's big leagues, but in most cases, they do it to escape the mundane rules that govern their everyday lives.

We will talk about carnivals, YMCAs, the military and veterans' organizations and the roles each played in making wrestling a part of mainstream America. We will talk about how the grandiose visions of one man took down an entire alliance that ruled the sport like the Mafia and how it left a state that had been filled with wrestling for over sixty years barren with inactivity. In turn, a generation of promoters was inspired to fill this void with their own upstart promotions, attempting to return the sport in the state to the level of activity of its golden years. Along the way, you will meet an eclectic group of people who call themselves wrestlers and/or wrestling promoters. This is the story of the history of professional wrestling in Mississippi.

PART I

EARLY DAYS

1

BEGINNINGS

Wrestling has existed since ancient times, appearing in nearly every early society. Some civilizations used wrestling to train their militaries while others staged matches during festivals and other celebratory occasions. The influence of wrestling on Greek society was the most notable, as the sport played a significant part in the early Olympic Games. Greek boys were made to learn the rules of the sport, even if they had no desire to take part in the Olympics or similar events. In the Americas, wrestling was a part of life for many Indigenous tribes. Like the Greeks, many tribes trained their children to wrestle from an early age. Though Native Americans embraced wrestling and other combat sports, they did not regard them as highly as did Europeans.

Early wrestling matches in Greece took place in a sandpit. There, wrestlers covered in oil and dust began in an upright lockup and attempted to pin their opponent's shoulders, hip or back to the ground. This style most resembles modern Greco-Roman wrestling. Around the time of the Renaissance, variations began to develop in England, where wrestling had become the most popular sport. These styles of wrestling differed in the way the matches opened, how they were won and what holds were legal. The most notable of these styles, "catch-as-catch-can," came into prominence in Lancashire County in northern England.

In catch wrestling, a fall is won by either pin or submission, and the winner of a match is the one who wins two out of three falls. This style of wrestling, unlike some earlier forms, had no system for awarding points to combatants. It also introduced the idea that a match may end in a draw between combatants. Many people see catch-as-catch-can wrestling as the genesis of freestyle amateur wrestling, mixed martial arts and modern professional wrestling.

The sport was not immediately popular with early European settlers in the northeastern portion of what is today the United States. Many of these early settlers were Puritans, who believed that sports were frivolous and bad for society. It took until the late 1600s in the southern and central colonies for the idea of sporting events to gain popularity. During this time, wrestling matches were scheduled during festivals and used to resolve conflicts. Three U.S. presidents were frequent wrestlers: George Washington, Abraham Lincoln and Zachary Taylor. Of these, Lincoln was the most accomplished, as he was a great practitioner of the collar-and-elbow style popularized by Irish immigrants in Vermont. Though these highly influential men engaged in the sport, wrestling was a favorite of the common people, as other sports, like horse racing, were open only to the upper class.

Another aspect of sports in the United States involved slavery. Plantation owners often pitted their slaves against one another in contests such as footraces, ball games, wrestling and boxing to entertain themselves and other wealthy planters in their company. Oftentimes, these men placed large bets on the outcome of the events. In some cases, plantation owners knowingly stirred up trouble among their slaves to create the need for a boxing or wrestling match.

William Muldoon, who practiced the Greco-Roman style, was the first superstar of wrestling. He was born between 1845 and 1852 in rural New York. His peak years were from the late 1870s until his retirement in 1891. Muldoon was a model of physical fitness and chose to abstain from alcohol and tobacco. It was with Muldoon that wrestling took its first step toward what we know today as professional wrestling. He put together a group of strongmen, wrestlers and boxers and toured cities across the United States. In a carnival-like atmosphere (and with charged admission), the public was invited to engage in wrestling, boxing and multidisciplinary matches with Muldoon and members of his troupe. To entice them to participate, the audience was offered prize money if they could last a certain amount of time with the fighter. If no one accepted the challenge, Muldoon engaged in "worked" matches with other members of his troupe. *Worked* is a term in wrestling that means "rehearsed or predetermined." This was the beginning of the carnival era of professional wrestling, which would be almost completely replaced by organized wrestling exhibitions by the mid-1920s.

William Muldoon.
Library of Congress.

Beginning in late 1888, Muldoon helped train boxing's World Heavyweight Champion John L. Sullivan for his fight with Jake Kilrain, a man handpicked by Sullivan's enemies to take his world championship. Muldoon and Sullivan had known each other since the early 1880s, when Muldoon helped the "Boston Strong Boy" break into boxing. The Sullivan-Kilrain fight paid the winner $25,000, an unheard-of amount of money at the time. The two fighters also placed $10,000 side bets on themselves.

This highly anticipated match was fought on July 8, 1889, in a field in Richburg, Mississippi, in Lamar County. A crowd of at least three thousand people made its way to the fight's location, which was unknown to all but a select few. Secrecy was necessary, because prizefighting was illegal at the time and Governor Robert Lowry was doing his best to make sure the fight did not happen. Despite his best efforts, the fight did occur, and a bloody affair it was. It lasted an exhausting seventy-five rounds—more than two hours—with Sullivan besting his opponent. After the fight, both men fled Mississippi quickly, only to be arrested in other states for their illegal actions. Each man ended up serving a few months in jail. Sullivan was fined $500 for his role in the fight, and Kilrain was fined $200. This bout was the last notable match to use the London Prize Ring Rules, which involved bare-knuckle fighting and allowed takedowns.

The Kilrain fight was not the first in Mississippi for Sullivan, and it was not his only run-in with Governor Lowry. On February 7, 1882, Sullivan captured the American Heavyweight Championship from Paddy Ryan on the yard of the Barnes Hotel in Mississippi City, near Gulfport and Biloxi. The fight ended after nine rounds, but Sullivan manhandled Ryan for most of the match. Many onlookers feared for Ryan's safety during the match. One witness was quoted: "That boy from Boston is liable to kill a man with a blow."

While the two men were training for the fight on the Mississippi Gulf Coast, they received word that the Mississippi legislature was working on a bill to make prizefighting illegal in the state. In response to this news, the two men and their entourages fled to Louisiana, but they found themselves unwelcome there as well. Thus, the combatants, along with two thousand spectators from around the country who had traveled to see the fight, headed back to Mississippi and Ryan's training headquarters in Mississippi City for the bout. While Governor Lowry had urged the Harrison County sheriff to not allow the fight to happen, the lawman was conveniently occupied elsewhere that day. This fight kicked off the series of events that would cement Sullivan's legacy as the most prominent fighter of his time.

The first documented organized professional wrestling matches in Mississippi took place only a few years before these pivotal boxing matches, in December 1884. The matches were between "America's Champion" Professor Will Willie and German ex-champion Professor Burnstein. It is likely that neither man was actually the academic sort, though that is only educated speculation. The match was probably with Greco-Roman rules, as this was Will Willie's specialty. Though almost nothing is known about Willie, he appears to have been one of the most prolific grapplers of the late 1800s. The men faced off at Vicksburg's Magnolia Hall and Robinson's Opera House in Jackson. There were several other matches held in Vicksburg later in the 1880s and '90s, making it the first hotbed

Drawing of John L. Sullivan. *Library of Congress.*

of wrestling activity in the state. Perhaps this explains why this city has produced so many important figures in the history of wrestling in the state.

Just as Sullivan ushered out the era of bare-knuckle boxing, the popularity of Greco-Roman wrestling waned with Muldoon's retirement. In its place as the preferred style of wrestling in the United States was the more brutal catch-as-catch-can wrestling, which began to dominate the grappling landscape in the early 1890s. Though this type of wrestling more closely resembles today's professional wrestling, it was still quite different from what we see today. Instead of a ring, catch fighters in the nineteenth century fought on either grass or rock-covered fields. By the early twentieth century, when the likes of George Hackenschmidt and Frank Gotch had become icons of the sport, matches took place on unforgiving floors covered only in cloth. Though the sport still looked vastly different, it was during this time that the foundation would be laid for what would become the billion-dollar industry we know today.

2

WRESTLING IN THE EARLY
TWENTIETH CENTURY

By the early 1900s, athletic clubs had begun to pop up in many larger cities and towns in Mississippi. These clubs often hosted exhibitions featuring wrestling, boxing, baseball, basketball and footraces. The athletic clubs were often connected to a city's Young Men's Christian Association buildings. They provided entertainment for festivals and other special events during that time. On one occasion, the Tupelo Athletic Club scheduled wrestling matches to entertain a crowd of five thousand people who had gathered to watch a man be hanged for the Amory murder of a family of four. The occasion made headlines across the nation, including in New York City and Kingstree, South Carolina.

Some schools scheduled field days during this time that included many of these newly popular sports. The traveling carnival wrestling that had been popularized in the state beginning in the 1870s and 1880s was also still going on at this time. In carnival wrestling, a carnival champion would take on any audience member willing to fight him. In this form of wrestling, the idea was that the challengers would never win, but sometimes they did, causing conflict at times. One such case occurred in 1917 in Vicksburg and involved professional wrestler Young Sandow, not to be confused with Billy Sandow of the famous Gold Dust Trio. Sandow issued an open challenge to the audience, which was accepted by local wrestler Mallick Joseph. Much to Sandow's chagrin, he was unable to pin Joseph's shoulders to the mat in the promised five minutes. Joseph said he would have done even better in the match had there been sawdust under the ring canvas. The practice was popular in wrestling during this time, as it supposedly allowed wrestlers to work faster. The two men met in another match in the following days, and they got into a brawl when Sandow refused to pay Joseph the five dollars he had promised for wrestling him again. The carnival's manager, a Mr. Barfield, ended up compensating the local.

During this period, wrestlers and other carnival workers developed a language to communicate with one another that only they could understand. Until the late 1980s, wrestling was a closed society. Men and women who entered the business were expected to keep its secrets, as wrestling was the livelihood of most of those involved. To ensure that a person could be trusted, those training wrestling hopefuls often tested their students' devotion to the cause by inflicting tremendous amounts of pain on them. It was not unusual for blood to be shed and even bones to be broken during the "initial training sessions." If the student was able to endure the pain and keep coming back, the trainers and promoters knew the person cared enough about the business to keep its secrets and to take care of the person they were working with in the ring.

Besides Vicksburg, Hattiesburg and Gulfport were two of the first cities in Mississippi to semi-regularly schedule events featuring wrestling outside the carnival or "sports program" setting. On Saturday, October 26, 1907, at the Auditorium Theater, Hattiesburg hosted a match between John Bonura and Young Hoyle for the "Middleweight Championship of the South." It should be noted that wrestling at this time was divided into weight divisions, much like boxing still is. This was commonplace until the mid-1900s, when the terms *heavyweight*, *light heavyweight* and, later, *cruiserweight* were the only ones frequently used. Bonura, known as the "Italian Whirlwind," was slightly more seasoned than Hoyle and had ten pounds on his opponent, while Hoyle was a clean-cut rookie generally adored by the crowd. According to Auditorium manager Mort L. Bixler, he had booked three wrestling events at the building the previous year, and they had been successful. He praised the virtues of wrestling, describing the sport as "clean" and "respected." The Auditorium Theater stood at the corner of Forrest and Front Streets.

In the years immediately following the Bonura-Hoyle fight, Gulfport hosted multiple wrestling matches. Often, the shows were based around Billy Morales, an inexperienced local lightweight. His opponents included Harry Mell, John McMahan (not the famous collar-and-elbow wrestler from Vermont) and a wrestler called "The Unknown," proof that colorful monikers began popping up early in professional wrestling. These matches were held at George Pierce's Air Dome at the corner of Fourteenth Street and Twenty-Sixth Avenue. The open-air venue hosted vaudeville shows for about a year at the time of the matches.

With the exception of perhaps Professor Will Willie, three-time Southern Middleweight Champion Peter James was the first national star to wrestle regularly in the state. The Greek expat first appeared in Mississippi on Wednesday, May 17, 1911, at the Walnut Street Theatre in Vicksburg, winning matches over both Young DeRoona and Paul Polk. James also wrestled on Thursday, August 24, 1911, at Pierce's Air Dome against Young Hackenschmidt. The Hackenschmidt name was a nod to "The Russian Lion" George Hackenschmidt, arguably the most popular wrestler at the time. James won the match in two straight falls going approximately forty minutes. This event was notable because the opening matches included a boxing match and a "battle royal" featuring many different boxers in a free-for-all. Boxing and wrestling were often featured on the same card through the mid-twentieth century. "Danish Fox" Bob Farrington and Ed Sterling also wrestled in Gulfport in 1911. Farrington was promoted as the undisputed Southwest Middleweight Champion. In a match between Farrington and Young Hackenschmidt, the *Biloxi Herald* noted that the audience wasn't very large, as people they called "knockers" had been telling others that the match would not be legitimate. The *Herald* stated, "If there was a streak of yellow anywhere it did not show up during the evening."

In 1914, another Hackenschmidt, Leo, toured the state. This alleged cousin of George defeated local blacksmith Jas W. Evans at the Brookhaven Opera House on Thursday, March 26, and again a week later at Woodmen Hall in the city. He fought California wrestler Joe Thomas at the Jackson Fair Grounds on Thursday, May 7, and then traveled north to Macon to challenge resident Jerre Clark, who won amateur titles in Illinois and Indiana.

Peter James returned to Mississippi on Tuesday, May 28, 1912, to lose a match to the Middleweight Champion of the South, Joe Cutrer, at the Majestic Theatre, No. 2, in Jackson. This was the name of the former Gem Theatre after Houston Bowers, proprietor of the original Majestic Theatre, acquired the building. Cutrer, Vicksburg's Mallick Joseph, former police officer William Sheehan (Vicksburg), Henry Furr (Lincoln County) and J.L. Mashburn (Columbus) were the first Mississippi-born wrestling stars in the state. Cutrer was born in Osyka, a tiny town in Pike County, and attended Mississippi A&M, the previous name of Mississippi State University. Cutrer was still wrestling in the South by 1916, when he gained wins over K.I. Simmons in the Pike County town of Magnolia in February and Henry Furr in March at Woodmen Hall in Brookhaven. Furr was a Lincoln County farm boy who gained respect as a wrestler by defeating "The Terrible Swede" when Dreamland Shows came through Brookhaven in November 1915. Furr was still wrestling in 1922, when he defeated carnival wrestler Gustave Hanson twice at Brookhaven's Fish & Untz Skating Rink in November of that year.

Wrestling in Mississippi also grew because it was a popular activity with military men at bases throughout the state in the early twentieth century. At Camp Shelby in Hattiesburg, wrestling and boxing bouts were held almost weekly, beginning in 1917, and exhibitions for the public were held on special occasions. According to the camp newspaper, *Trench and Camp*, "The interest in boxing and wrestling [was] great [during this time]." By 1918, many servicemen were appearing in boxing and wrestling matches at the Knights of Columbus Hall in Hattiesburg. Soon, the Gulfport Naval Training Station joined the Hattiesburg base and began boxing and wrestling matches of its own.

Organized wrestling events also began to pop up across the northern portion of the state. Grenada hosted its first wrestling match on March 5, 1919. Two military champions squared off in the ring. Jack Harwood from Charleston, Mississippi, the navy champion, defeated army champion Al Athan, two falls to one. According to the *Jackson Daily News*, this win gave him the "Championship of the Middleweight."

The previously mentioned Columbus lightweight J.L. Mashburn began to gain momentum on November 12, 1919, when he defeated "Bull" Smith, a carnival wrestler from the visiting Patterson Shows. Professor Rex, a Pennsylvania wrestler residing in Tupelo at the time, was unable to pin Mashburn twice in an hour during their match at the Columbus Opera House on Thursday, April 22, 1920. Mashburn returned to the venue on Monday, August 2, to face Victor Kalfus from Pensacola, Florida, in a match sponsored by the American Legion. Kalfus, like Rex, could not pin Washburn twice in one hour. On Monday, September 14, 1920, a series of American Legion–sponsored matches began to happen in Columbus featuring Mashburn, Kalfus, Polish Middleweight Champion Mike Nestor and Jack Ross, who was holding the Southern Middleweight Title that Peter James had defended in the state in 1911. These matches were held regularly for a few months. Kalfus also wrestled a match in Ackerman against Young Zbyszko at the Gem Theatre on July 4, 1921, and against an unknown opponent in Jackson on March 18, 1922.

The string of wrestling shows in Columbus that had been sponsored by the local American Legion, along with a host of Vicksburg matches sponsored by the city's Volunteer Southrons Legion, were some of the earliest partnerships between veterans' organizations and this growing sport in the state. These relationships grew and were a huge part of the sport in the Magnolia State through the 1980s. Along the way, other groups, such as Lions and Rotary clubs, Parent Teacher Associations and police leagues would begin partnering with local wrestling events. Many wrestling events today partner with community groups for fundraisers or to raise money for medical bills for designated individuals. This spirit of philanthropy began in the state in the mid-1920s with historic promoters like Billy Romanoff and Earl McGrory.

In October 1923, wrestling challengers of an entirely different variety visited the state capital. They came with the Hagenbeck Circus, and each of the five competitors weighed around five hundred pounds. Yes, these fearsome fighters were some of the first wrestling bears in the United States. Unlike later bruins that would come through, the public was not invited to try their luck with the creatures from this circus. Instead, onlookers were content to enjoy exhibitions between the mammals and their trainers. In the 1980s and early '90s, bear wrestling was a phenomenon in some nightclubs around the United States until several animal-rights groups spoke out against the practice. Around the time the first wrestling bears began to appear in the state, carnival wrestling began appearing much less frequently. In their place, men began arriving in cities and towns attempting to stage regular matches there and in surrounding areas. This is the format that dominated professional wrestling until the 1980s, when a handful of national organizations would take over the wrestling world.

3

THE ROMANOFF YEARS

The year 1925 set the stage for professional wrestling to reach great popularity in Mississippi for the first time. In that year, Clarksdale began hosting wrestling events at least once a month, usually at the Strand Theatre, sponsored by the American Legion and promoted by Tennessee-born boxing and wrestling promoter Earl McGrory. Clarksdale would continue to host frequent matches, most often on Thursday nights through the mid-1930s, and these included a veritable who's who of heavyweight wrestling talent of the era. Some of the most notable were past, reigning or future World Heavyweight Champions Ed "Strangler" Lewis, Stanislaus Zbyszko, Joe Stecher, Jim Londos, Jim Browning, Wayne Munn, Pete Sauer and Orville Brown. Other marquee names appearing in the "golden buckle on the cotton belt" included Joe "Toots" Mondt, Dick "Rough Richard" Daviscourt, George Zaharias and Rudy Dusek. These big names were likely able to appear in Clarksdale so often because of the city's proximity to Memphis, where these heavyweights would often wrestle for promoter/wrestler Charlie Rentrop. Rentrop also wrestled in Clarksdale quite a bit himself around this time, which further suggests that he was heavily involved.

Clarksdale played host to the first documented masked wrestler in Mississippi, the Masked Marvel, in 1926. This gimmick was used quite often around the country by a host of different wrestlers and was briefly played by Pete Sauer in Clarksdale. The first documented all-women's match in Mississippi also took place at the Strand in Clarksdale, as Teddy Myers went over Rosa Stein on December 21, 1927.

Other towns in the Mississippi Delta, such as Greenville, Itta Bena and Indianola, also hosted wrestling events in the mid-1920s. The Indianola events were held in a building that had recently been used by Millender & Davis, a dry-goods store. These cities were generally unable to attract the big names that Clarksdale did, most often featuring wrestlers like Charlie Rentrop and Boris Demitroff. The most notable match of this period happened in Indianola and was the first documented intergender wrestling match in the state. Surprisingly, this matchup seemed to predate any female-on-female fights in the state by over two years. The 1925 match pitted Dorothy Apollo, described as a "muscular amazon," against Jack O'Neil. Apollo had vowed to "throw," or pin O'Neil's shoulders to the mat, twice within an hour but was ultimately unsuccessful. Apollo did

Stanislaus Zbyszko was one of the most accomplished wrestlers of the early twentieth century. The former world champion was one of several historic grapplers who appeared in Clarksdale in the 1920s. *Wikimedia Commons*.

gain the first fall, but O'Neil was able to pin her shoulders to the mat after using a hammerlock to take her down in the second. Because Apollo lost that fall, the match was over and awarded to O'Neil. As most wrestling fans know, intergender matches have become quite frequent only over the past ten years, mainly in independent wrestling circles. Any intergender matches before that were usually gimmicky bouts featuring a woman taking on a manager perceived as a weakling. In the northeastern part of the state, veteran wrestler Victor Kalfus hosted a handful of matches in Columbus in the first few months of 1926.

Shifting one hundred miles south to the capital city of Jackson, a welterweight wrestler named Billy Romanoff came into town in 1925 and there found a home for the rest of his life. He would become a staple of the wrestling scene there as a promoter for nearly thirty years, the first ten of which he was also an active in-ring competitor. Romanoff would help Jackson surpass Clarksdale by the 1930s as the wrestling capital of the Magnolia State, a distinction it enjoyed until at least the late 1970s, when Biloxi and Tupelo began to have their own cases for that distinction.

Billy Romanoff may have been born Wilhelm Heinrich Meyer on January 25, 1891, in Dielingen, Germany, as a petition for naturalization filed in

Jackson on September 3, 1953, states. On the 1940 census, however, he already lists himself as a naturalized citizen. Stranger still, the 1950 census lists his birthplace as Nebraska. In the ring, he presented himself as a relative of the former Russian royal family (Romanov). It is hard to determine if he was actually born overseas or if he carried on an elaborate ruse most of his life to lend an air of authenticity to his wrestling persona.

What is known about him is that he began wrestling by 1913 and had matches across the Southwest and Midwest before coming to Jackson in November 1925. Interestingly, he was billed as being from Omaha, Nebraska, in many matches prior to arriving in Mississippi. Romanoff held Pacific Titles in both the Middleweight and Welterweight Divisions. Other names Romanoff wrestled under include William Meyer, Young Meyer and Young Romanoff.

As a wrestler, Romanoff was said to be a skilled technician, and he was described as a "master of psychology" as a promoter. He went the extra mile to make wrestling fans believe the things they saw were real. Today, this is called keeping "kayfabe." In one instance, a muscular young wrestler billed from Hungaria named "Tarzan" Al Szasz was being brought into the Jackson area to wrestle. Romanoff made sure his audience believed the billing with a clever, if perhaps crazy, publicity stunt. Romanoff sent a scantily clad Szasz into a Jackson residential area with instructions to climb a few trees. Romanoff proceeded to call the police and tell them that a wild man was on the loose. The police picked up Szasz and took him to jail, where Romanoff was waiting to explain the situation. The public had a field day with the story, just as Romanoff intended. In another trick, still used sometimes today, Romanoff sent wrestler Buck Lawson's young son into the ring to shed a few tears over his fallen father. Doctors then rushed in to check on Buck after he took a body slam from Middleweight Champion Gus Kallio.

Jackson would host a few of the same world-renowned heavyweights in Clarksdale during that time, but crowds in the capital city seemed to prefer the faster working styles of lighter wrestlers. This may have been because Romanoff became very popular in the state and, while still an active competitor, was able to bring in wrestlers of a similar size to serve as his opponents. Some of the most notable wrestlers who appeared in Jackson during the mid-to-late 1920s were Alfred "Dutch" Mantell, World Welterweight Champion Jack Reynolds, World Middleweight Champion Gus Kallio, Mexican Indian Yaqui Joe, jiu-jitsu master Matty Matsuda, "Terrible Turk" Ali Hassan and Joe "The Wild Bohemian" Kopecky.

Kopecky was known for spitting tobacco in the eyes of his adversaries. Alfred "Dutch" Mantell should not be confused with his namesake, who debuted in 1972 and made his own mark in wrestling in the South and across the nation. The original "Dutch" was a Luxembourg-born heel who nearly incited riots during many of his matches. Each of the hundreds of matches Romanoff booked in the state capital over the next three decades was sponsored by the Henry H. Graves Post of the American Legion. Most of these events were held at the City Auditorium, though matches in warmer months were often held outdoors in either the ballpark (in the 1920s) or in one of the open-air arenas on Pearl Street constructed in the 1930s exclusively to host these events.

Vicksburg continued to be a wrestling hot spot at this time, though not as much is known about activities there. The city hosted a match in January 1926 featuring Joe Stecher, recognized World Heavyweight Champion. He lost to Boris Demitroff, who was billed as the Bulgarian champ, in a match in which neither title was on the line. Vicksburg shows continued to be held intermittently during the years immediately following that big match. The Henry Lammons American Legion Post of Yazoo City voted to start hosting wrestling matches in July 1926. These were held at the Ideal Theatre Building on Main Street, on a vacant lot beside City Hall and at the American Legion Stadium on Broadway Street at various times between 1926 and 1927. Yazoo was able to occasionally host top-tier talent appearing in Clarksdale, like Jim Browning, Dick Daviscourt and George Sauer. Boxing was more popular than wrestling in Gulfport in the 1920s, though the city hosted some wrestling matches with boxing affairs. The coast did not fully embrace wrestling until the mid-'30s. Meridian is thought to have been another major city for the sport. It held a match in January 1927 at the Shrine Mosque in which still reigning champion Joe Stecher beat "The Balkan Bear" Dan Koloff in two straight falls. This match was promoted by Lucien Morrow, who was a part of Meridian's American Legion. Meridian held events each Tuesday at the Open-Air Arena from late 1931 through 1933. Wrestling matches were also held in Appolonia, Belzoni, Carthage, Corinth, Crystal Springs, Laurel, Natchez, Pascagoula and Union around this time.

The American Legion Posts of McComb and Greenwood expressed interest in holding wrestling events in the mid-1920s, but they did not act on this interest immediately because of uncertainty regarding the legality of boxing and wrestling. Citing the legislation passed thirty years earlier that outlawed "prizefighting," Attorney General Rush H. Knox issued an opinion in 1927 stating that wrestling and boxing were "absolutely against the criminal laws of the state of Mississippi." Representative William T. Wynn responded by helping author a bill that called for wrestling, sparring and boxing to be legalized and for the creation of a state athletic commission to regulate them. The bill was not popular with everyone, as some feared that the legalization of these activities would cause widespread gambling and moral corruption. On March 29, 1928, Governor Theodore G. Bilbo signed the bill, which the American Legion had vigorously advocated for, into law. A 10 percent tax was placed on "all theater, college and school athletic exhibitions, wrestling, sparring, and boxing match tickets." The first State Athletic Commission was composed of Chairman R.B. Morrow of Brandon, Luther Maples of Gulfport and Harry J. Landry of Friars Point. Landry would go on to have a huge impact on wrestling throughout the United States in the 1930s and '40s.

Even though the idea of wrestling and boxing was still fairly new to the area, it did not take long for the sport to endear itself to the state's citizenry, specifically those in Jackson and Clarksdale. The Jackson *Clarion-Ledger* called wrestling "one of the favored sports in the city." It also said that the sport was "growing in popularity among the men and women in the city," calling it an "interesting and even thrilling affair." It was a part of many major events in a town, such as fairs, events that still have some crossover with professional wrestling to this day. Attendance for most of Jackson's bigger wrestling crowds in the 1920s stayed around two thousand.

One of the most influential people in wrestling throughout the nation in the 1930s and '40s was the previously mentioned Harry J. Landry. After the National Wrestling Association was created from the National Boxing Association in 1931, he was elected president of the newly formed organization. The National Wrestling Association should not be confused with the National Wrestling Alliance, which was formed in 1948 and ruled the wrestling landscape through the 1980s and still exists in a diminished form today. During his decade-plus tenure heading the National Wrestling Association, Landry was credited with carrying out almost all of the organization's actions. Landry, who was born in New Orleans, was a colonel in the Mississippi National Guard, a former mayor of Friars Point and a former multi-term supervisor for Coahoma County. He was also an accomplished businessman, as he ran an insurance agency and was the president of Exchange Bank in Friars Point. He passed away on January 2, 1955, while in Memphis, Tennessee, and most of his contributions to the sport have been largely forgotten.

Besides a ten-month period in 1931 when he went on his last tour as a wrestler and the occasional short breaks at the end of "seasons," often taken during the winter and late summer / early fall, Romanoff's Jackson wrestling events were a constant in the state until the mid-1950s. During his 1931 hiatus, the sport was absent altogether from Jackson for seven months. When it returned later that year, the matchmaker was Jack Groves. Programs there during Groves's tenure leaned more toward heavyweight fighters, with a special appearance by Jim Londos, as well as more frequent appearances by wrestlers such as Marshall Blackstock and Tom Malloy. The audience vocalized its preference for the faster-paced matches Romanoff had promoted. When he came back and retook the reins the next year, he would not vacate that role for more than twenty years.

During the 1930s, Romanoff's shows included many of the same wrestlers he had used in the previous decade, but many others made their debut in the area during that time. Among these new additions were U.S. Navy veteran and legitimate tough guy Sailor Moran, future National Wrestling Association World Heavyweight Champion Sandor Szabo, World Light Heavyweight Champion Leroy McGuirk, "Wild" Red Berry, Navajo Indian Chief Little Wolf, Texas technical wrestler Rex Mobley, Farmer Grove from Meridian, The New York Jewish Sensation Ace Freeman, Chinese jiu-jitsu practitioner Chin Lee, Louisiana's Farmer Mack, "French Trapper" Jean LaBelle, Oklahoma "master of the flying head scissors" Balk Estes, Japanese jiu-jitsu star Sugy Hayamaka, "Tarzan" Al Szasz, Buck Lawson, "Irish" Paddy Nolan, "Cowboy" Jack Purdin and "Gentleman" Jack Curtis. Curtis, a young Vicksburg native, was the first wrestler in a family that would leave the largest mark of anyone on the sport in the state of Mississippi. By this time, Jackson shows were being held almost exclusively on Friday nights, where they would stay for the overwhelming majority of Romanoff's career.

In addition to Jackson, Romanoff began supplying promoters in other towns with talent in the mid-1930s, creating what is now known as the Jackson Booking Office. The first city to book wrestlers through Romanoff was Gulfport, which would grow to be the second-biggest wrestling city in the state in the 1930s and '40s. Matches were held on Wednesday nights there at an outdoor arena on Thirty-Sixth Avenue beginning in May 1935 and at the indoor Legion Arena in the colder months. The coastal city would host matches throughout most of Romanoff's tenure. H.S. "Tony" Everts, a longtime legion member, most often promoted Gulfport's shows during that period. By September 1937, Romanoff had expanded his empire yet again by promoting events at Legion Stadium in the Delta town of Greenwood.

Kid Harris, the matchmaker there, tried hosting a few shows at Greenville's National Guard Armory before deciding to concentrate on Greenwood. Greenwood hosted shows throughout the 1930s and considerably fewer shows in the '40s. Romanoff also revived matches in Yazoo City at the Fairgrounds Arena and also hosted them in McComb for a short period in the late 1930s. Pascagoula promoter Adolph Thomas held a series of cards at that city's American Legion Arena with both wrestling and boxing in the late 1930s. In these years, Clarksdale flip-flopped several times among promoters and weight classes but would use mostly Romanoff's talent through the 1940s with local promoter Les Chapman.

In the northeastern portion of the state, Batesville, Columbus and Oxford are known to have hosted wrestling events in the 1930s. Corinth was the biggest wrestling hot spot in this part of the state at the time. Several different venues were used for shows there, including two different buildings at the fairgrounds and, later, the Hinton Chevrolet Building. Many of the same wrestlers who appeared in other parts of the state also worked Corinth shows. Some of the most frequent competitors there were Roy Welch, Freddie Knichel and George Ligosky. In an unfortunate turn of events, a wrestler named Eddie Baker lost his life in a Corinth ring on May 14, 1937, at the age of thirty-six. He had suffered a heart attack in his main event match with Welch, never coming up after being pinned by his opponent. Welch was likely promoting many of the Corinth shows by the late 1930s. He was a hard-nosed wrestler who had been trained by Alfred "Dutch" Mantell. Welch moved from his home state of Oklahoma to Dyersburg, Tennessee, and began taking over wrestling in surrounding towns, often using forceful tactics. It is also likely that Welch promoted shows in other North Mississippi towns around this time. In 1935, a *Clarion-Ledger* article stated that Romanoff was planning to bring wrestling to Tupelo's "American Legion Casino." No documentation of these matches has yet been found, and it appears that Tupelo was more of a boxing town at the time. It is likely the American Legion Casino was merely the downstairs portion of the organization's building, where its members were known to play cards and had slot machines until they were destroyed by a tornado in 2014. Officially, these slot machines were for "entertainment purposes only."

One notable outdoor wrestling show in the northeastern part of Mississippi took place on November 10, 1930, in Columbus. The promoter for this match was a man named Arch Persons, a scheming young Alabama native. In one moneymaking endeavor, Persons convinced boxing's ex–Heavyweight Champion Jack Dempsey to appear as a special referee for a wrestling match he booked. Persons had met Dempsey when the former boxer was having an affair with his wife. Persons expected as many as 11,500 people for the event, and he went all out in promoting it as "Jack Dempsey Day" in the city. Unfortunately, Mother Nature had other plans, and a major storm barreled down on Columbus that day, keeping all but 3,000 people from attending. Persons was unable to pay all the expenses incurred in promoting the event, such as the cost of bringing in the wooden bleachers. Dempsey even found himself being sued by Mose Winkler of Meridian, who supplied the bleachers for the event. In an interesting side note to the story, Persons and his often-unfaithful wife had a child together in 1924 and divorced in 1931. Persons's wife soon would remarry, this time to a wealthy Cuban expat named Joe Capote. Capote adopted his new stepson, Truman. Truman, of course, went on to write *In Cold Blood*, a true-crime classic published in 1966.

For a few months at the end of 1937, Jackson had two different wrestling programs: Romanoff's American Legion–sponsored light heavyweight / middleweight show on Fridays and a Veterans of Foreign Wars–sponsored heavyweight show on Thursdays. Colton Skidmore, a former boxer, was in charge of promoting the new events. Both shows were featured at Jackson's City Auditorium. Among the wrestlers spotlighted on the Jackson heavyweight shows were Douglas Wyckoff, a former All-American lineman from Georgia Tech; Chief Little Beaver, a Native American from the Pacific Coast; Dr. Karl Sarpolis, the master of the nerve hold; and Texan Juan Humberto. The VFW brought a young Lou Thesz to Jackson when they briefly revisited their heavyweight program in 1938. If there was any competition between the two promoters or the two veterans' organizations, it isn't apparent. Skidmore ended up being a referee for Romanoff for many years after this, suggesting that any animosity between the two was short-lived.

As in the 1920s, many new ideas were first explored in Mississippi in the 1930s. Some of these ideas were quite silly; others continue to be a major part of the sport today. The first battle royal–type event in Mississippi took place at Jackson's City Auditorium on January 26, 1934. At that time, it was known as a "wrestle royal," because it was based on boxing's battle royal concept of fighting until only one combatant remained standing. Instead of a modern battle royal with over-the-top-rope eliminations, the only way to eliminate an opponent in a wrestle royal was by pinfall. After only two competitors remain in a wrestle royal, they would meet in a single match later that night The participants in the first wrestle royal were Freddy Kupfer and Andy Tremaine, who often wrestled in Jackson during that period, and lesser-known wrestlers Jack Hogan, Bobby Carney and Joe Sandusky. It wouldn't be until a few decades later that battle royals began resembling the modern versions.

This idea was turned comical on April 10, 1936, with the first "blindfold rassle royal." Each participant was said to have had their eyes taped and "stockings over their heads." The match was won by Otto Ludwig and Roy Welch, who went on to face each other in the evening's main event. Other participants in the match were Benny Matthews, Verne Clark, The Red Flash and Schoolboy Knox. Surprisingly, the blindfold idea is still revisited from time to time. Kenny Valiant, Mississippi promoter and wrestler from the 1980s through the 2010s, occasionally hosted blindfold battle royals on his shows, though no stockings were involved. Valiant says that the crowd loved yelling directions at their favorite wrestlers to help them locate their opponents.

On a card held in Jackson on Christmas Day 1937, a greased-pig match was held between "Irish" Paddy Nolan and Sailor Watkins. In such matches, both men were rubbed down with axle grease before wrestling. I'm sure it was fun to watch, but I can see why it didn't catch on. Several mud matches were also held between wrestlers during this time. Those types of matches eventually gained popularity, but not with traditional wrestling fans. Instead, mud wrestling popped up mostly in bars and nightclubs and generally featured scantily clad women before a mostly male audience in what many consider an exploitative practice.

The first modern handicap match in the state took place at Jackson's City Auditorium on April 8, 1938, when the 640-pound Martin "Blimp" Levy simultaneously battled a quartet of wrestlers: Roy Reynolds, Tex Riley, Ernie Arthur and Bobby Sampson. One man had faced multiple wrestlers in the same night dating back to the carnival days, but everything up to this point seems to have been done in a gauntlet style, with one wrestler facing multiple wrestlers in a series of singles matches. Levy was one of the first wrestling "attractions" to come through the state. Attractions were wrestlers with unusual physical characteristics, such as exceptional height or weight, whom people might pay to see out of curiosity. This builds on the same idea behind the circus "freak show." Attractions were a big part of wrestling through the 1980s—longer, in some instances.

The most common match type today outside of the standard singles contest is the tag team match. This type was first tried in Mississippi in 1938, in Jackson. On Friday, July 1, the team of Cyclone Burns and Frankie Hill wrestled to a draw with Sailor Adam and Dick Sampson. The match was well received, with the *Clarion-Ledger* writing, "[The tag team match] proved such a success here…that [Billy Romanoff] can sit back and rest on his glory and give fans more of the same." Romanoff was not the first to stage this type of match anywhere, but he may have been one of the earliest adopters of the match, depending on which origin story you believe. Some say that the first tag matches occurred as early as 1901, with Joe Stecher and his brother, but this has not been proven with documentation. The first documented tag team match was held in Houston, Texas, on October 2, 1936, less than two years before Romanoff began using the idea. He began holding six-man and eight-man tag team matches in 1939 and 1950, respectively. For his time, Romanoff was a daring promoter who was not afraid to try new things to keep audiences coming back week after week.

The 1940s and early '50s strongly resemble the first half of Romanoff's run in the Magnolia State. Light heavyweights were still dominating the state at the time, and the Mississippi/Louisiana version of the World Light Heavyweight Championship was the title most sought after in this region. "Gentleman" Jack Curtis was arguably the most successful wrestler in the state at the time. From 1942 to 1952, Curtis held that coveted title at least nine times. Besides Curtis, holders of the title who appeared in the area included fellow Vicksburg-area native Henry Harrell, Rex Mobley, Jack "Stinger" Steel, Balk Estes, Bobby Segura, Walter "Buff" Sirois, Jack McDonald and others. Other important workers in the territory at the time were Jack Curtis's half-brother and frequent tag team partner George (Culkin) Curtis, Leo Jensen, Al Getz, Sailor Parker, "The Louisville Comet" Floyd Byrd, Bob Castle, Dutch Schultz and Flash Clifford.

Besides events happening in Jackson and Gulfport, J.L. Snellgrove, who wrestled under the name Farmer Grove, began booking matches in Meridian and Hattiesburg by the early 1940s. The Hattiesburg matches were closely associated with the Camp Shelby Army Base and sponsored by the Lacy Kelly VFW Post and, later, the Disabled American Veterans. Snellgrove frequently held matches in these cities through the mid-'40s. The Harry Harvey Legion Post would also resurrect wrestling for a few years at the end of the 1940s, holding matches at the McComb National Guard Armory. After years of editorials expressing a distaste for the sport and many false starts, Greenville briefly got back to hosting wrestling matches in 1949. Camp Shelby in Hattiesburg and Keesler Field Air Force Base in Biloxi also held many matches during these years featuring active military men and occasional touring professional wrestlers.

On July 18, 1948, a group of prominent wrestling promoters met in Waterloo, Iowa, to devise a coalition to take back control of the sport from two men, Tom Packs and Paul Bowser, who were the respective managers of the National Wrestling Association and American Wrestling Association World Champions. In controlling the two champions, Packs and Bowser had tremendous power and could make sure that the champions spent most of their time defending the titles in the areas where they promoted. The group created at the Iowa meeting was called the National Wrestling Alliance (NWA), and it would largely control the sport for the better part of forty years. In the meeting, the promoters created a set of operating procedures for the group and its collective championships. The procedures were meant to prevent any one promoter from gaining too much power while also ensuring that members of the group would not attempt to sabotage one another's operations. The alliance also created a (mostly) undisputed World Heavyweight Champion and allowed member promoters to easily swap talent with other members. This allowed promoters to create new feuds in their territories and keep their audiences from becoming bored with overused wrestlers. As a result, nearly every notable wrestler came through the state once the NWA was in place there. Whether for good or ill for Jackson and the entire state of Mississippi, neither Billy Romanoff nor any lesser-known Mississippi promoter of that period was in Iowa that day. In fact, Romanoff would never be a member of the National Wrestling Alliance. It wasn't until 1955, when he vacated his position atop the Mississippi wrestling world, that the alliance made its entrance into the state.

As the 1950s arrived, the consistent wrestling city of Hattiesburg began hosting matches again, this time at Greater Hattiesburg Park, the Hattiesburg Community Center and, later, the Livestock Show Grounds. Other cities and venues for wrestling shows between 1951 and Romanoff's exit from the business in 1955 included Anguilla (Legion Arena), Biloxi (Gulf Coast Boxing Arena and Pass Road Speedway Arena), Forest (High School Gymnasium), Greenwood (Carrolton Arena), Greenville (Frisby Stadium Ballpark), Kosciusko (Whippet Gym), McComb (Palace Theater), Mount Olive (Mount Olive Gymnasium), Pascagoula (Pascagoula Recreation Center on Market Street), Rolling Fork (High School Gymnasium), Winona (National Guard Armory) and more. Though many of these events featured wrestlers who were often associated with Romanoff, it was clear from the assortment of new wrestlers and towns that the business was growing beyond Romanoff. In the 1950s, wrestlers such as Brookhaven's Big Boy Cronin, Gulfport's Pat Newman, Charlie Laye, Wild Bill Steddum, Tiger

Moore, "Irish" Jack Kelley, Joe Corbett, Chief Apache, Johnny Harmon, Dangerous Danny Dusek and a young charismatic blond named Jackie Fargo frequently appeared on the state's wrestling cards.

Along with his lightweight wrestlers, Romanoff and other Mississippi promoters brought in frequent "attractions" from the late 1930s onward. At this time, women's wrestling was considered one of these attractions, not the integral part of the mat game it has become over the past twenty years. The most famous lady grappler of the 1930s, '40s and '50s, World Champion Mildred Burke, made her first of many trips to Mississippi on June 15, 1939, when she wrestled Gladys Gillian in Pascagoula at the American Legion Theatre, which had also been known as the Nelson Theatre. While most of Mississippi seemed to appreciate women's wrestling, not every city here welcomed these grappling gals. The Greenwood American Legion Athletic Commission canceled the appearance of two females in the squared circle there in 1938. A statement from the commission quoted in the *Greenwood Commonwealth* reads, "A woman's place is in the home or some place other than the local wrestling arena." The commission said it canceled the event because it feared criticism for allowing women to participate in such an "unladylike" activity." Other lady grapplers who wrestled in the state during Romanoff's tenure included early African American lady wrestlers Babs Wingo and Kathleen Wembly, "colorful hillbilly" Elvira Snodgrass, future World Wrestling Federation (WWF) star Mae Young, Ann Miller, Velma Jordan, Dolly West, Juanita Cauffman, Ann La Verne, Millie Stafford, Therese Theis, Cora Combs and June Byers.

Another big attraction that came to Jackson in the early years was former AWA World Heavyweight Champion "The French Angel" Maurice Tillet, who wrestled in the capital city on February 10, 1950. He had appeared all over mainstream media in the 1940s. Tillet was essentially the precursor to

"The French Angel" Maurice Tillet (*front, center*) in 1936. *Wikimedia Commons.*

Andre the Giant. Like Andre, Tillet had acromegaly, a condition that causes the pituitary gland to release too much growth hormone. In his teens, Tillet's hands, feet and chest grew at a tremendous rate. After his incredible size led him to abandon his dream of practicing law, he entered the professional wrestling world in 1936. By the time he visited the Magnolia State, his career was in its twilight. As you can imagine, promotional materials for his visit were very cruel, calling him the "world's ugliest man" and a "close specimen to the cave man." It is rumored that Tillet was the inspiration for Dreamworks' Shrek character, but that has never been substantiated. However, there is certainly a resemblance between the two.

Cowboy actor Sunset Carson made several appearances in Jackson in 1949, refereeing matches and doing his trick-shooting act during events' intermissions. Primo Carnera, the former World Heavyweight Boxing Champion, wrestled in Jackson and Meridian in 1950. The first documented "midget" wrestlers came to Mississippi on Friday, April 27, 1951. Appearing in the first match of this type were Sky Low Low, Pee-Wee James, Sonny Boy Cassidy and Fuzzy Cupid. Other attractions coming through the state around this time included the flamboyant "Gorgeous" George Wagner, Goliath from the film *David and Bathsheba*, Ada Ash wrestling an alligator and a handful of wresting bears.

PART II

A NEW ERA

4

THE NATIONAL WRESTLING ALLIANCE COMES TO MISSISSIPPI

The year 1955 was the end of an era for wrestling in Mississippi, as Billy Romanoff sold his promotion and booking rights in the state to Roy Welch in February. Welch had promoted and wrestled throughout the Southeast since the 1920s and had likely been booking some shows in the northern part of the state already. Welch and his partner, Nick Gulas, joined the National Wrestling Alliance in 1949. Once Welch took over for Romanoff, he began to run shows in Jackson at the famous City Auditorium, Greenville at the Armory on Poplar Street and then the Walnut Street Arena, Biloxi at the Pass Road Speedway Arena, Gulfport's Legion Arena, Vicksburg's Legion Arena and Greenwood's Legion Baseball Park. Among the wrestlers who appeared on shows in the mid-'50s were Roy Welch's son Buddy Fuller; Roy's brothers Herb and Lester Welch; Roy's nephews Bobby, Don and Lee Fields; the villainous Mario Galento; World Junior Heavyweight Champion Baron Michele Leone; Southern Junior Heavyweight Champion Sonny Myers; "Rowdy" Red Roberts; Ray Piret; Ali Pasha; a young Eddie Gossett (Graham); Don Wayne; Eddie Malone; Rube Wright; Charly Keene; Killer Karl Kowalski; Stan Kowalski; second-generation Mississippi wrestler Jack Curtis Jr.; lady wrestlers Dot Dixon, Belle Starr, China Mira, Lana Lamar and Millie Stafford; and "midget" wrestlers Lord Littlebrook and Ivan the Terrible. Wrestlers who remained active in the state from Romanoff's tenure included Rex Mobley, Jack and George (Culkin) Curtis, Eddie "Buff" Sirois, Danny Dusek, Charlie Laye and Henry Harrell. In 1955, Jackson's City Auditorium wrestling matches began to be shown on Jackson's WJTV with McComb native Robert Nickey serving as the show's announcer. From that moment forward, television and Mississippi wrestling would be intertwined.

Welch ran shows in the area quite frequently that first year, but the shows became less frequent after that. By the end of May, cards began to pop up featuring mostly wrestlers made famous in the state during Billy Romanoff's tenure, as well as a few new faces. A May 27, 1956 *Clarion-Ledger* article described one of these events as "rebel type wrestling," and the City Auditorium was even referred to as the "Rebel Wrestling Arena" for a short time. Jackson favorites who appeared at these shows included wrestlers such as the Curtis Brothers, Wild Bill Steddum, "Irish" Paddy Nolan and "Tarzan" Al Szasz. Newer faces like Nelson Royal, Johann Von Brauner, Magnolia State police officer turned wrestler Earl Guess, Frank Hurley and The Golden Terror also appeared with this group. Top lady wrestlers of the day, such as Slave Girl Moolah (later The Fabulous Moolah) and Judy Grable, also appeared on some of these shows. Besides Jackson, this group ran events in Columbia, Greenville, Greenwood, Hattiesburg, Magee, Natchez, Newton and Vicksburg. A March 21, 1957 article states that Earl Guess was a promoter with a group fronted by the Curtis Brothers, who had purchased promotional rights from Roy Welch. The wrestlers on these events were generally the same as those featured when the "rebel wrestling" term began to be used, but it is unknown whether the two were one and the same.

Three weeks after "rebel wrestling" debuted, Mississippi mainstay Rex Mobley began booking wrestling shows at the Jackson Auditorium on Tuesday nights under the auspices of the Southern Wrestling Alliance. Mobley's events featured most of the wrestlers who worked Welch's shows there, plus others like World Tag Team Champions Corsica Joe and Corsica Jean, Charley Carr, Johnny James, "Gorgeous" George Grant, Prince Omar Khyam, Don Miller and Ivan Zaukov. This company ran events in many of the towns run by the rebel group, as well as coastal cities like Biloxi and Ocean Springs.

These two organizations often ran shows on the same nights in cities that were geographically close, but never the same cities on the same night. The only example of possible animosity between the two occurred on Wednesday, June 19, 1957, when the two groups ran shows with different lady wrestlers, both of whom claimed to be "The Lady Angel." One Angel was promoted as the "world's ugliest girl wrestler" and was said to make "women faint" and "children cry." Rex Mobley booked his angel in Columbus that night, and rebel wrestling booked theirs in Natchez. On the subject, the *Hattiesburg American* quoted Mobley: "Mine is the real one. She's baldheaded and from Europe. The other one, she's just a girl who shaved her head." The paper also quoted George Culkin, whom the paper listed as promoting the rival event: "Aw, phooey. It's just the other way around."

By the fall of 1957, all signs of Mobley's Southern Wrestling Alliance were gone. During this time, Roy Welch continued occasionally running Northeast Mississippi towns. Roy's son Edward "Buddy Fuller" Welch began running the Gulf Coast territory, which included the Mississippi cities of Biloxi, Gulfport, Laurel and Hattiesburg, with occasional "spot" show towns like Columbia, Ocean Springs and Wiggins. The rest of the state continued to host mainly cards with Romanoff-era stars, though the era of weekly Jackson City Auditorium shows during this time ended. The group of older stars occasionally booked shows in the iconic building, as did Lee Fields, who purchased the Gulf Coast territory from his cousin Buddy Fuller in 1959, but he never seemed to gain any real momentum in the city. Besides the usual cast of Welch/Fields characters, "Fabulous One" Jackie Fargo and his kayfabe brother Don, arrogant antihero Sputnik Monroe, tremendous technical wrestler Billy Wicks, Joe Scarpa (the future Chief Jay Strongbow in the WWWF), Jack Curtis's sons Randy and Jack Jr. and others worked for Gulf Coast Championship Wrestling (GCCW) in the late 1950s. In February 1962, promoters began holding events at the Agricultural Building at the State Fair Grounds in Jackson, the first sign that the old City Auditorium's days were numbered.

In the early 1960s, several non-NWA-affiliated, or "outlaw," wrestling promotions began to pop up in the state. The most interesting of the "outlaw" shows at that time happened on Wednesday, July 19, 1961, at the Star Theatre in Hattiesburg. The event was the first documented card in the state to feature only Black wrestlers. It featured a mixed tag team match with Ramona Isabella and Speedy Williams against Babs Wingo, who had appeared in the state almost ten years prior, and The Black Panther. This was the only card advertised in the *Hattiesburg American* for this group. Though Black wrestlers had appeared in wrestling for decades, this card showed that there was a large audience of African American people interested in attending wrestling events. Wrestling, like other sports, would play a tremendous role in bringing people of all races together. Before integration, wrestling matches, like most other public events, had a section designated for "colored people." This section was often in the balcony or in the back of a building. White wrestler Sputnik Monroe helped integrate the sport in nearby Memphis by appealing to promoters' love of money. He had gained tremendous popularity with the Black community in Memphis, so much so that not all who came to the matches could fit in the designated "Blacks only" area. Pointing out the amount of revenue the company lost by not letting African Americans purchase standard tickets at the Ellis Auditorium, Monroe was able to persuade them to open up all tickets to everyone. Unfortunately, this idea did not immediately spread south to Mississippi. The state was among the last to fully integrate, with some areas not doing so until 1970.

A man named Peter Giannopulos ran an outlaw promotion called Rebel Championship Wrestling (RCW) in the mid-1960s. He operated throughout most of the state, even running events at Jackson's City Auditorium. His cards featured the likes of longtime Mississippi wrestler Wild Bill Steddum, veteran wrestlers Hercules Mcintyre and Prince Omar, rookies Tennessee heel Don Gaston (later Don Carson) and Mississippi technical wrestler Billy Hamilton, as well as Mississippi-born lady wrestler Jean Atone and veteran lady star China Mira. This company was the first in Mississippi to embrace the idea of branding, as RCW shows were easily distinguishable from the crowd. The advertising for most promotions at that time, including those by Welch and Fields, often generically referred to wrestling events as "Professional Wrestling" or "Championship Wrestling." Welch's flyers often featured the line "Wrestling—King of Sports."

Speaking of Welch and Gulas's territory, it is worth mentioning that Tupelo's favorite son and the original King of Memphis (and rock 'n' roll) was a wrestling fan. Elvis Presley often attended matches at Ellis Auditorium, shielded from the view of the public. Between 1957 and 1958, Elvis even briefly dated lady wrestler Penny Banner. According to Jerry Lawler, Elvis's connection to the sport did not end there. According to the other "King," plans had been discussed regarding a possible martial artist versus wrestler match at the Mid-South Coliseum. According to Lawler, he and Elvis's dad, Vernon, discussed the idea twice, and Vernon reported that Elvis was interested in the idea. The discussions took place in 1977, and the proposed match was considered for after Elvis got in shape for and completed his tour. As we all know, fate had other plans. Presley died on August 16, 1977.

By the 1960s, Welch and Gulas were bringing several shows back into Corinth, Mississippi, at the Fairgrounds Ball Park and the American Legion Building at the fairgrounds with Leonard Fielding as the local promoter. They likely ran other cities in the state then as well, such as Clarksdale, Columbus and perhaps even Tupelo. Some of the wrestlers featured in these events included tag teams Corsica Joe and Corsica Jean, villainous

German cousins Karl and Kurt Von Stroheim, the masked Mexican duo The Black Monsters and Carlos and Pete Caruso. Singles wrestlers included "Rowdy" Red Roberts, Chief Kit Fox of the Comanche tribe, Spanish Light Heavyweight Torbellino Blanco, Treach Phillips, Joey Corea, Tiny Santana, Fritz Hess, Tony Lorenzo, Gene Dundee (later Flash Monroe) and "midget" lady wrestlers Darling Dagmar and Baby Cheryl. It should be noted that, for a long time, wrestling took advantage of public perception against certain groups. As a result of World War II, the evil German or Japanese heel was a lasting trope in the business at that time, and evil Russians and Middle Easterners also gained in popularity. The 1960s and '70s was the heyday of masked wrestlers, particularly in Gulas's and Fields's territories. Most often, masked wrestlers of the period played the roles of heels, perhaps because the masks dehumanized them and made it harder for the crowd to relate to them. Besides the typical masked gimmicks of the day (Destroyers, Infernos, etc.), the Welch and Gulas territory of the 1960s and '70s often included characters based on Hollywood movie monsters, like The Mummy and Dr. Frank (Frankenstein's monster). North Mississippi's Melvin Kimball played the part of The Mummy for Welch and Gulas in the mid-'70s.

By early 1964, Lee Fields had stopped running shows on the Mississippi Gulf Coast regularly. Instead, he focused on the Alabama and Florida coast for a few years. Some smaller shows were scheduled in 1965 and 1966, including a few at the City Auditorium in Jackson and weekly shows at the Stock Barn in Forest for a few months. The shows included the likes of Jack Curtis Jr. and Randy Curtis, Sonny Cooper (Don Jardine / The Spoiler), "The Great Mephisto" Frankie Cain (an important character in Mississippi wrestling history a little later), Hawaiian wrestler Oni Wiki Wiki, Earl Guess, Starkville's Charles Putt, Chuck Bowman, Bill Currie, Duke Scarbo and female wrestlers Margie Ramsey and Peggy Allen. Many of these same wrestlers also began appearing on weekly shows that promoter E.J. Myrick started on Friday, November 4, 1966, at a building called The Barn at 1411 Thirtieth Avenue in Gulfport.

On Monday, December 14, 1966, a skating rink in Greenville called Skate-o-Rama began hosting wrestling events for Nick Gulas and Roy Welch. In early 1967, Gulas and Welch shows also began popping up elsewhere in the state, including several appearances at the Greenwood VFW with local promoter C.H. "Roundman" Nolan and at the Eupora National Guard Armory sponsored by the Eupora Lions Club. Featured wrestlers included Corsica Joe, Rocket Monroe, Dwayne Peal (future Buddy Wayne), Ed Younger (young "Plowboy" Frazier), Al "Spider" Galento, Larry Dean,

Mississippian Jerry Dean (future Rip Tyler), Tim Tyler, Bobby Whitlock, Sonny Scott, "Big" Jim Holly, Ray Lopez, Young Anaya, Fred Bass (later famous Memphis manager Sam Bass), The Scufflin' Hillbillies (Rip Collins and Chuck Connelly), Jerry Loveless, Rick Neal (Ricky Fields), The Cuban Assassin, Black Jack Dillon and others.

By 1967, Gulas and Welch had begun holding matches in Tupelo at the Fairgrounds Community Center. The "All-America City" would become a weekly town for the territory by January 1969. A young promoter named Jerry Jarrett, whose mother had worked for Welch and Gulas since the 1940s, was the one booking shows in Tupelo at the time. Herman Sheffield worked as the local promoter for most of these shows. Wrestlers appearing at these early fairgrounds shows included Jackie Fargo, Mario Galento and popular babyface "The Tupelo Kid" Bob Arnold, who came from Memphis to live in Tupelo in 1967 and enjoyed a long career working for the Lee County Sheriff's Department. Also among these wrestlers were Japanese stars Shinja Kojika, Motoshi Okuma and Mitsu Katayana; young Tennessee wrestler Lavon Stone; mat veteran Danny Dusek; Native American Chief War Eagle; the masked Golden Terrors; Dr. Frank; Black Death; Jo-Jo Sumo; Danny Lee; Abe Griffith; Gene Garcia; Roughouse Barry Gordon; Jose Morella; and lady wrestlers Sylvia Hackney and Ann Jeanette. The company also ran spot shows as far south as Philadelphia's Choctaw Community Center, where a show was held on Friday, March 8, 1968.

Lee Fields brought his Gulf Coast Championship Wrestling promotion back to the Mississippi Gulf Coast in March 1968 and began showing weekly wrestling on WDAM Channel 7 in Laurel on Saturday afternoons from 5:00 to 5:30 p.m. and on WLOX in Biloxi on Saturday nights from 10:30 to 11:00 p.m. Wrestlers who began working for Fields in the late '60s and often wrestled in Mississippi included Cowboy Bob Kelley, who would become the most popular wrestler across the Gulf Coast, and tag teams The Dirty Daltons—Jack (Don Fargo) and Frank—and Bad Boy and Billy Boy Hines. There were also masked heels The Blue Yankees, "Outlaw" Eddie Sullivan, Mexican star Jose Lopez, Kenny Mack, Cobra Kid, Maxie York (Ricky Morton's uncle), Billy Spears, Don Sharp and Jessie Venegas. Throughout the 1970s, Mississippians like Jerry Perry, Ray Rowland, Melvin Kimball, Aaron Holt, Roy Justice and others worked around the Gulf Coast and throughout Mississippi.

My father relayed a story to me that I feel perfectly illustrates the absurdity of the relationship between professional wrestling and real life. Like many wrestlers, Mr. Perry was a truck driver when he wasn't in the ring. He worked

Left: Jerry Jarrett is the promoter who brought Memphis wrestling to Tupelo. He was also one of the company's most popular wrestlers in the 1960s and '70s. *Kathy Hinds Moore*.

Right: The Fabulous Fargos: Don (*top*) and Jackie (*bottom*). *Wikimedia Commons*.

with my father at Malone and Hyde, a wholesale food distributor based in Tupelo. He and my dad became friends and often spent nights at the same truck stop, where Mr. Perry would relay humorous stories about his days in the ring. As one of the masked Red Destroyers, Perry was a heel, which meant that the fans often berated him. One fan in particular stood out to Perry. Perry knew this fan, but the fan had no idea that he knew the dastardly Red Destroyer. During the week, this fan was a shipping supervisor at a pickle factory in Wiggins, a common pickup location for Malone and Hyde drivers. Perry was sent to this factory often to pick up a load, and he and this shipping supervisor would carry on friendly conversations. Never could Perry mention the secret weekend meetings between the two, as that would break kayfabe, the code that wrestlers lived by in those days to protect the business and their livelihood by ensuring that fans thought the business was as real as possible.

George (Curtis) Culkin, who retired from the ring in 1960 and spent seven years as a deputy sheriff in his home of Warren County, began booking wrestling events around Vicksburg, Greenville and Jackson in the late 1960s. In 1968, he decided to pursue this full-time. To finance this venture, Culkin sold 123.4 acres of his previously 127 acres of land. Culkin would use wrestlers for his shows from Leroy McGuirk's NWA Tri-State promotion, which was already running Oklahoma, Arkansas and Louisiana. By 1969, Curtis was running everywhere in Mississippi except the extreme north and south of the state. His early towns included Jackson, Vicksburg, Greenville and Natchez, as well as spot shows around the state, such as at McComb's National Guard Armory and Kosciusko's Attala County Fairgrounds as a part of the Central Mississippi Fair. In 1970, all Jackson wrestling events moved to the Coliseum at the Mississippi State Fairgrounds, effectively ending an era. The demolition of the City Auditorium began that same year. In April 1971, Culkin added a weekly show in Greenwood at the new Sportatorium, a building that he had constructed on Highway 49 South for that purpose. The most sought-after title in NWA Tri-State was the North American Heavyweight Championship. Wrestlers who came to Mississippi in the early days of the McGuirk/Culkin partnership included North American Heavyweight Champions like "Crazy" Chuck Karbo, superb amateur wrestler Danny Hodge, Tarzan Baxter and The Spoiler (a masked heel who would be a mainstay in the territory for years). Also included was "Cowboy" Bill Watts, a tough Oklahoma wrestler and shrewd businessman who would soon gain a partial stake in the company. And there was the cunning heel Skandor Akbar. Other stars for the promotion in the late 1960s and early '70s included Culkin himself, who came out of retirement for several months in the late '60s; Culkin's nephew Jack Curtis Jr.; rookie Gerald Brisco; veteran Antonio "Argentina" Rocca; Memphis antihero Sputnik Monroe; vicious heel Ox Baker; burly big men Grizzly Smith, Klondike Bill and Luke "Big Boy" Brown; Gorgeous George Jr.

"Cowboy" Bill Watts (*left*) with The Crusher. Watts began appearing with Leroy McGuirk's NWA Tri-State promotion in the 1960s and eventually bought into the company. In 1979, he split from McGuirk and founded what became Mid-South Wrestling and the Universal Wrestling Federation until the sale of the latter in 1987. *Wikimedia Commons.*

(not related to the original Gorgeous George); 600-pound Man Mountain Mike; 475-pound Haystacks Muldoon; Pancho Villa; Japanese stars Chati Yakouchi, Matti Suzuki and Mr. Ito; the deceptively named "Gentleman" Jerry Miller; African American star Tom Jones; "Cowboy" Ron Reed (later Buddy Colt); heel "Dandy" Jack Donovan; German Karl Von Stroheim; Spanish star Juan Sebastian; Russian Nikita Mulkovich; Canadians "Cowboy" Frankie Lane and Jerry London; Native Americans Chief Kit Fox and Danny Little Bear; Jim Osborne (future Dr. X); Jim and Frank Dalton; The Mummy; Mexico's Pedro Valdez; and veterans Oni Wiki Wiki, Frank "Gorilla" Marconi, Treach Phillips and Sundown Kid.

By the mid-'70s, the Culkin / McGuirk-Watts partnership was enjoying good crowds at every town they worked. Nearly every big star in wrestling made appearances in Mississippi for Tri-State at the time. Some of the wrestlers who would spend a portion of their earlier careers here were future main event stars like Texas brawlers Stan "The Lariat" Hansen and Frank Goodish (Bruiser Brody), future "Million Dollar Man" Ted DiBiase, the flamboyant "American Dream" Dusty Rhodes, Sylvester Ritter (who became the most popular star in the territory as Junkyard Dog), second-generation, old-school heel Greg "The Hammer" Valentine, Olympic strongman Ken Patera and Bob Slaughter (Sgt. Slaughter), along with solid workers like Japanese star Kazuo Sakurada, Troy Graham (Dream Machine), madman "Killer" Tim Brooks, Black stars Bobo Brazil and Porkchop Cash, "Captain Redneck" Dick Murdoch, Hiro Matsuda, Toru Tanaka, Killer Karl Kox, Waldo Von Erich, Ivan Putski, "Bruiser" Bob Sweetan, "Hippie" Mike Boyette, "The Angel" Frank Morrell, Billy Robinson, Larry "The Axe" Hennig, Ronnie Garvin, Buck Robley, Danny Miller, Mississippi's Rip and Randy Tyler (Randy Rice) and John Tolos. Superstars like Harley Race, Terry and Dory Funk Jr. and Andre the Giant would also make occasional appearances in Mississippi for the group. According to promoter Gil Culkin, George Culkin's son, crowds were great during this time. For an event headlined by a cage match pitting "Cowboy" Bill Watts against Dr. X, 9,700 people showed up. Though attendance records for wrestling events are often not made public and there is no official record, my research suggests that this is the most people to ever attend a wrestling event in the state.

In 1972, Jerry Jarrett's father-in-law, wrestler Eddie Marlin, purchased the booking rights for Northeast Mississippi, including Tupelo. Along with Tupelo and North Mississippi, he also booked several towns in surrounding states. This allowed him to quit his day job at a rubber factory. Jarrett had started wrestling himself in 1965, having been trained by veteran Sailor Moran and Tojo Yamamoto, a major star in the territory. He had also become an integral part of Welch and Gulas's office. In 1973, Jarrett left the territory to become a booker for Jim Barnett's Georgia Championship Wrestling in Atlanta. While Jarrett helped Georgia soar, his home territory's crowds began to shrink. To help the territory thrive again, Gulas and Welch were able to lure Jarrett back by giving him a 10 percent stake in the company and waiving the previous fees that had been charged to book "his" towns. Not too long after that, Welch became sick, and Jarrett had the opportunity to purchase another 40 percent of the company for $50,000.

Promoter and wrestler Eddie Marlin was Jerry Jarrett's father-in-law. He was the promoter in Tupelo during its most prosperous years. *Kathy Hinds Moore.*

In 1970, a cartoonist-turned-wrestler named Jerry Lawler, who would eventually earn the nickname "The King," made his debut in the ring. Lawler was in demand all across the Gulas territory, and crowds in North Mississippi either loved or loved to hate him, depending on what his character was doing at the time. Joining lynchpins Jarrett, Marlin, Yamamoto and Lawler in the early '70s were the still-popular Jackie Fargo and his clan, beloved tag team star Tommy Gilbert, African American star Bearcat Brown, Len Rossi, Jimmy Kent, journeyman veteran Oni Wiki Wiki, the underrated Frank Hester, Jim White, an iteration of The Samoans, Karl and Kurt Von Brauner, The Original Heavenly Bodies (Al and Don Greene), Roy Welch's grandson Robert Fuller, Welch's nephew Jimmy Golden, The Bounty Hunters (David and Jerry Novak), Lorenzo Parente, Sonny King, Northeast Mississippi natives Melvin Kimball and Aaron Holt, managers Saul Weingeroff and Sam Bass and others.

With Welch beginning to have a firm grasp on the northeast portion of the state, Fields having success booking the southern portion and George Culkin establishing his wrestling empire almost everywhere between the two, there wasn't much room for anyone else to attempt to run wrestling in Mississippi. However, this didn't mean that it was impossible. One group, Southwestern Championship Wrestling, set up shop in McComb at the National Guard Armory, with former Hattiesburg policeman James (Bill) Baylis running the show. They also eventually promoted regularly in

Wrestling fan Kathy Hinds Moore takes a photo with Jerry Lawler at the Tupelo Sports Arena. *Kathy Hinds Moore.*

Mendenhall and tried their hand at promoting in Hattiesburg alongside Gulf Coast Championship Wrestling shows. These shows generally featured an equal mix of men's and women's wrestling, even sometimes including intergender matches. A good portion of their wrestlers had generic names and gimmicks: The Avenger, The Black Diamond, The Cajun Queen, The Apache Indian, The Big Yankee, The Little Yankee, The Mad Russian, Masked Maggie, The Fugitive, Seminole Gene, Cowboy Knight, Madam X, Bad Boy Taylor, El Toro, The Blonde Bomber, Black Angel, The L.A. Hippie and The White Phantom. These shows were halted on Wednesday, November 27, 1973, when Baylis died from injuries sustained in an automobile accident. The shows returned to McComb in February 1974 and eventually ended up under the promotion of a man named Charles Dunaway. The matches lasted only through that summer. Another notable "outlaw" company at the time was called Mid-South All-Star Productions, which ran shows at Louisville's A.A. Hathorn Recreation Center with Charlie Rice as promoter. Its shows featured "Tiny" Frazier, Larry Latham, The Interns and Junior Rice (Randy Rice in a full hillbilly getup as Frazier's partner). Ring veteran Lavon Stone also had a promotion that ran shows in Corinth's American Legion in the late 1970s.

In 1977, change was on the horizon again for pro wrestling in Mississippi and around the southern United States. Nick Gulas was attempting to "push," or build up wins, for his son George in an attempt to elevate him into the main event. From many accounts, George was uncoordinated, and fans did not get behind him. When Jarrett refused to allow George to be booked in his portion of the territory, Gulas let Jarrett know that Jarrett didn't actually own anything and that he had only purchased an option to buy into the company, and that window had passed. Furious at hearing this, Jarrett struck out on his own, creating the Continental Wrestling Association (CWA) on February 14, 1977, taking most of the talent with him from his collaboration with Gulas. After Roy Welch passed away later that year, Buddy Fuller joined Jarrett, and the two created the Jarrett-Welch Wrestling Company. The two joined the National Wrestling Alliance in 1978 but left by 1979 and began recognizing their own "World" champion. Tupelo and Eddie Marlin would stay with Jarrett and become a big part of the territory through the late 1970s and early '80s.

Through the '70s, Tupelo shows would move among several venues. After starting at the Fairgrounds Community Center in the late 1960s, the shows moved to the Westmoreland Sports Arena, then briefly across town to the Natchez Trace Hall of Fame and finally to the Tupelo G&M Sports Arena on Broadway Street. It is the latter for which Tupelo would be most remembered. Though many of the events there were iconic, the building was certainly not aesthetically pleasing. The converted garage had no air-conditioning or heat and only enough seating for about five hundred people at most. While the building was more primitive than venues like Memphis' Mid-South Coliseum, it had the advantage of allowing fans to interact more closely with wrestlers, often carrying on conversations with them and taking photos with them. On one stormy Friday night in 1978, the Tupelo Sports Arena was forced to be even more primitive. Conditions had caused the lights to go out in the building. Rather than close the show and refund people's money or suspend the show with hopes that it could be resumed later that night, the rollup door of the old garage building was raised, and promoter Eddie Marlin pulled his pickup truck to the door and shined his headlights on the ring. The rest of the night was finished this way. What makes this story even more surreal is that the storm that caused the power outage was not just any storm, but a tornado that pulverized the city's McRae's store approximately a mile from the arena.

It was also inside this small, no-frills arena that one of the most famous matches of all time would occur: the Tupelo Concession Stand Brawl. The date was June 15, 1979, and Memphis wrestling was in a bad spot. Robert Fuller had just left Memphis as the booker and had taken most of the roster with him. The main event featured Southern Tag Team Champions Jerry Lawler

The Tupelo Concession Stand Brawl jump-started the career of Wayne Farris. He went on to dye his hair black and become the Elvis-impersonating Honky Tonk Man. Honky is the longest-reigning WWE/WWF Intercontinental Champion of all time, holding the belt for 454 days in the late '80s. *Kathy Hinds Moore.*

and Bill Dundee against the recently arrived tag team The Blonde Bombers, Wayne Farris (Honky Tonk Man) and Larry Latham (Moondog Spot). The two teams were asked to have a match that brought down the house, and it certainly did. After the Bombers won the title, the former champions sought revenge, and the fight broke out that would lead into the concession stand. Nearly everything in the stand, including food, condiments, boxes, glass and anything else in sight, was used in the fight. The brawl was filmed and shown on Memphis TV the next morning, and a sensation was created. Business was booming in the territory for the next few months because of this. Allegedly, Herman Sheffield, the local promoter who ran the concession stand, told everyone beforehand that anything in the stand was fair game except the popcorn machine.

As with anything that is successful, the concession stand brawl was copied many times over the years. The third Tupelo Concession Stand Brawl featured the young team of Eddie Gilbert and Ricky Morton against Japanese wrestlers Atsushi Onita and Masa Fuchi. In 1989, Onita opened a new promotion back in Japan called Frontier Martial-Arts Wrestling (FMW). This company would take the extreme violence shown in the concession stand brawls even further, featuring matches that often included barbed wire, broken light tubes and exploding tables. This promotion created a whole movement of hardcore wrestling and risky, violent "death matches" that continue today. Many people feel that Onita's time in Memphis and his involvement with that third brawl greatly influenced his decision to create FMW.

All the major stars of CWA, or "Memphis Wrestling," came through Tupelo in the late 1970s and early '80s. Some of the bigger stars in the territory were Lawler, Dundee, Tommy and Eddie Gilbert, Jimmy Valiant, Jos LeDuc, The Blond Bombers, Dennis Condrey, Austin Idol, Koko Ware, David Schultz, Plowboy Frazier, Rocky Johnson, Terry and Eddie Boulder

(Hulk Hogan and Brutus Beefcake), Mississippi-born manager Jimmy Hart, The Fabulous Freebirds, Hector Guerrero, Tommy Rich, Paul Ellering, Ricky Morton and Robert Gibson. Perhaps the only wrestler to be just as popular as Jerry Lawler in North Mississippi was Bill Dundee. Scotland-born and Australia-bred, Dundee came into the country and the territory in 1974 with fellow Aussie George Barnes, but Barnes decided to return home before long. Dundee, dubbed "Superstar," would win numerous titles and spend a large portion of his career in epic battles with Lawler. On an interesting sidenote, Rocky Johnson used to bring his young son "Dewey" to shows with him in Tupelo. Dewey grew up to be Dwayne "The Rock" Johnson. Many attending wrestling matches at the Tupelo Sports Arena have stories of meeting the young future superstar.

Elsewhere in the state, the Culkins had become the biggest wrestling presence because of their territory's large geographical area at that time. "Cowboy" Bill Watts had become the head booker for the promotion and handled most of the day-to-day operations. According to Gil Culkin, the original arrangement allowed the Culkins to pay the wrestlers in cash nightly

Young Eddie and Doug Gilbert often accompanied their father, Tommy, on his trips to wrestle in Tupelo. Both boys grew up to have successful in-ring careers and wrestle all over the state themselves. *Kathy Hinds Moore.*

for their matches. However, by the mid-'70s, Watts had asked them to send the money they would pay the wrestlers to the booking office, which would then pay the wrestlers weekly by check. Culkin says that many wrestlers began to complain that their checks were for less money than when they were paid by the Culkins directly. Also, by 1976, Watts and the Tri-State office decided they wanted to run towns like Greenville and Natchez monthly, instead of weekly, ostensibly because the towns were not drawing large enough crowds to be worth their time. These are two factors that created tension between the Culkins and Watts. So, when an opportunity arose, George and Gil were willing to consider parting ways with Watts and McGuirk.

In late 1976, Lee Fields began to slow down promoting wrestling because it was hard to balance that with running the Mobile International Speedway, which he also owned. The Culkins had learned that Fields planned to sell his territory to his cousin Buddy Fuller's son Ron (Welch) Fuller. Fuller had no interest in promoting wrestling in Mississippi at this time. Instead, he wanted to concentrate on Alabama, Florida and Tennessee. Thus, a deal was arranged that allowed George and Gil to purchase the rights to promote wrestling in towns in southern Mississippi formerly ran by Fields. This allowed the Culkins to host events in Biloxi, Gulfport, Hattiesburg, Meridian and numerous spot show towns. With their reach now going across all of state except for the northeastern portion, the Culkins decided to try their luck at promoting on their own. They opened International Championship Wrestling (ICW) in 1977, aligning with the American Wrestling Association (AWA) in late 1978 and recognizing AWA Champion Nick Bockwinkel as their world champion. "The Great Mephisto" Frankie Cain, a veteran wrestler who had known George Culkin for quite some time, was hired to be the company's booker. ICW's first television tapings were held in Greenwood at the Channel 6 studios in September 1977.

Program from an International Championship Wrestling event. *Gil Culkin.*

Watts was not willing to give up control of the steadily grossing city of Jackson, so NWA Tri-State and International Championship Wrestling engaged in the most intense territory war in Mississippi wrestling history. To help him compete, George's nephew and Gil's cousin Jack Curtis Jr. continued to work for Watts after the split, scheduling buildings and doing promotional work for the "Cowboy." As you can imagine, this put a strain on familial relations. However, Gil acknowledges that his cousin was making good money for Watts at the time and says he can understand why Jack didn't want to give that up, although it felt like an act of betrayal at the time. Watts did not find the battle easy, as the Culkins had built years of relationships in the state that helped them have leverage in the situation. ICW was able to take over the weekly Wednesday shows in Jackson, which alternated between the Mississippi State Fairgrounds Coliseum and the Industry Building on the fairgrounds site. Watts decided to run his shows on the exact day and time as ICW, but they were relegated to the inferior College Park Auditorium at the start of the war. By the summer of 1978, Watts had wavered and moved his events to Monday nights so he could go back to using the fairgrounds coliseum. For a few larger events, Watts even used Smith-Willis Stadium, the minor league baseball park in Jackson. The Culkins ran events all over the state, except for the northern portion, in cities including Biloxi, Greenwood, Greenville, Gulfport, Hattiesburg, Jackson, Laurel, McComb, Meridian, Natchez, Yazoo City and Vicksburg, and less often in towns like Indianola, Lexington, Magee, Magnolia, McClain, Mendenhall, Newton and Petal.

The roster for ICW included a mix of veteran wrestlers and unproven young talent. Most notably, several wrestlers who would become big names in the sport started their careers in the new promotion, including a sixteen-year-old Terry Gordy; his future Freebird partner Michael Hayes; James "Sugar Bear / Ugly Bear" Harris, who would be repackaged as Kamala, The Ugandan Giant, while wrestling in Memphis; journeyman territory worker Rip Rogers; and manager Percy Pringle, who would be most successful as The Undertaker's manager Paul Bearer in the WWF/E. It is also notable that ICW was the first and only promotion in the Magnolia State to host a reigning AWA World Heavyweight Champion, which the company did twice. Nick Bockwinkel took on African American superstar Porkchop Cash on November 15, 1978, at Jackson's State Fairgrounds Coliseum. Bockwinkel returned on Wednesday, March 14 of the next year to meet Mongolian #1. At different times, the core roster of the company included Gordy, Hayes, Harris, Rogers, Pringle, Cash, The Mongolians (Tio and Tapu), The Great Mephisto, Arman Hussein, "Pretty Boy" Ripper Collins, Oki Shikina, "Flying" Phil Watson, Dr. X , Johnny Mantell, Mr. Fugi, "Irish" Pat O'Brien, Tom "Boogaloo" Shaft, Tom Jones, Grizzly Smith, Troy "Hippie"

New Albany–born Ray Rowland was an accomplished wrestler, manager and promoter. Besides Ray Rowland, he also wrestled as a masked Intern, Colonel Ronnie Rowland (creator and manager of the original Ragin' Cajuns) and was a Fabulous Fargo Brother at one time. He appeared throughout the Southeast and eventually made his home in Columbus. *Tonya Rowland*.

Graham, Terry Lathan, Ricky Fields, Ken Dillinger, Sheik Zataar, Eddie Sullivan, Bill Ash, Nikita Alexev, Joey Rossi, Big O, Billy Screaming Eagle, Butcher Brannigan and Ozark Ike. Also included were Mississippians Gene Lewis, King Cobra, Thomas Tate, Ray Rowland and Ed Flukert and lady wrestlers Ann Casey, Cat Larue, Tracy Richards, Lily Thomas and Natasha. Other notable wrestlers who appeared in the territory included three-time NWA World Heavyweight Champion Lou Thesz, "Big Cat" Ernie Ladd, The Islanders (Afa and Sika), The Spoiler, Plowboy Frazier, Don Fargo, Norvell Austin, Don Bass, former NFL defensive end Verlon Biggs, Rip Tyler and Mr. Ito.

Watts and McGuirk mostly contained themselves to the Jackson area, although they did pop up elsewhere in the state from time to time. They also promoted their Loranger, Louisiana shows through the media in McComb, Mississippi. Along with some of his usual crew, other wrestlers for Watts during this territory war were such stars as Paul Orndorff, Len Denton, Thunderbolt Patterson, Jake Roberts, Ray Candy, Kevin Von Erich, Jose Lothario, Jerry Stubbs, The Assassin, Siegfried Stenke, Larry Booker (Latham), Carl Fergie, Kurt Von Hess, Prince Tonga (Haku/Meng), Ron Bass, Ron Slinker, Steven Little Bear, Bill Irwin, Superstar Billy Graham, Mr. Wrestling #2, Charlie Cook, Tank Patton, Baron Von Krupp, "Iron" Mike Sharpe, Mike George, Ali Bey, King Kong Mosca, Ivan Koloff, Ole Anderson, Hercules Ayala and Mike Bowyer.

The war lasted nearly two years, from October 1977 to August 1979. Culkin had brought a lawsuit against Watts, McGuirk and the NWA for running opposition to them in Mississippi while Watts maintained a monopoly on booking wrestling in the state of Louisiana. That state issued just one wrestling promoter license, and that belonged to Watts. George Culkin and Watts met in Jackson to discuss the lawsuit in the summer of 1979. As a result of the meeting, the two parties came to a settlement and agreed to resurrect their partnership. George's son Gil said he was "shocked," "angered" and "disappointed" by his father's decision. In his memoir, Watts claims that the Culkins' ICW was a failure and had actually folded prior to the lawsuit. Culkin adamantly disagrees with Watts on the way this all transpired and insists that the promotion was running quite efficiently before the agreement with Watts. From an outsider's view, ICW certainly did seem to have the upper hand in the war in Jackson. Instead of running ICW out of business by running in direct opposition to them, it was Watts who bowed out of the fight and moved to Mondays. While it is true that the Culkins' relationships with building management helped them gain leverage in the fight, that management would not have given preference to a company that was losing them money, regardless of personal relationships. In his book, Watts acknowledges that he "needed" to settle things with George Culkin. Whether this was to prevent himself from potentially losing money in the lawsuit or because he didn't think he could win the territory war is debatable. It was probably a mix of the two, as he says that it was the "best thing for both of them." Gil's memoir, *The Mississippi Wrestling Territory: The Untold Story*, details ICW's entire run against Watts and McGuirk, as well as Gil's other experiences in the business.

The first show for the renewed partnership between Watts and the Culkins was held on August 18, 1979, at Jackson's State Fairgrounds Coliseum. The company ran combined NWA/AWA shows for approximately a month, but on September 11, 1979, Watts dissolved his partnership with Leroy McGuirk and created the Mid-South Wrestling Association, with its headquarters now in New Orleans. The group would not apply for membership in the National Wrestling Alliance, although they did have talent-trading agreements with alliance members. Watts agreed to allow McGuirk to take Oklahoma, Arkansas and parts of Missouri and Texas, while he took Louisiana and Mississippi. Watts was content to book in only those two states until 1982, when he moved back into Tulsa and Little Rock, reestablishing most of the original Tri-State territory. According to Gil Culkin, the ICW roster was offered spots, but the only ones to accept were Porkchop Cash, Ricky Fields and Terry Lathan. He says that The Great Mephisto, James "Sugar Bear" Harris, Troy Graham, Izzy Slapawitz and Oki Shikina went to McGuirk's new split territory. Harris would return in a few short years as a main eventer for the promotion under his new gimmick of Kamala, the Ugandan Giant. In addition to Kamala, ICW alumni Terry Gordy and Michael Hayes would come back to Mississippi and work for Mid-South with Buddy Roberts as the famous trio The Fabulous Freebirds.

With the new partnership, most Mississippi towns were run sparingly. The newly uncontested Jackson was run most Wednesdays at the beginning of the new agreement, and Biloxi's Mississippi Gulf Coast Coliseum was also run most weeks. Greenwood shows were run monthly and moved to the Civic Center there. Meridian, Vicksburg and a few other towns were also visited during that time. Wrestlers who came to Mississippi in the early years of Mid-South Wrestling included Kerry Von Erich, The Iron Sheik, Wahoo McDaniel, Dizzy Golden, Gino Hernandez, Tommy Rich, The Masked Superstar (Bill Eadie, later "Demolition Ax"), Stan Stasiak, Tony Atlas, Buddy Landell, Bob Orton Jr., Austin Idol, Paul Ellering, Bob

Former NWA World Heavyweight Champion "Wildfire" Tommy Rich appeared in the state with CWA/USWA, CCW, Mid-South, WCW and many independent promotions. *Kathy Hinds Moore.*

Armstrong, Killer Khan, The Great Kabuki, Jimmy Garvin, The Samoans (Afa and Sika), Bob Roop, Bad Leroy Brown, Jonathan Boyd, Chick Donovan, Kelly Kiniski, Randy Rose, Terry Orndorff, "Crazy" Luke Graham, Frenchy Martin, Super Destroyer (Scott Irwin), Frank Dusek, Lars Anderson, Coco Samoa, Don Diamond, Ken Lucas, Tony Charles, Tugboat Taylor, Kim Duk and Jesse Barr. Lady wrestlers included Leilani Kai, Wendy Richter, Judy Martin and Judy Grable. While much of the state was dormant with this new arrangement, several small organizations, such as Tri-State Championship Wrestling and Hattiesburg Championship Wrestling, would pop up in the region. These shows would feature a combination of preliminary talent that had wrestled for the Culkins and/ or Watts and several wrestlers who had worked in smaller promotions like Southwestern Championship Wrestling and its offshoots. The promoter for Tri-State Championship Wrestling was Virgil "Speedy" Hatfield, the father of the Fields brothers and a referee for ICW.

PART III

WRESTLING'S PEAK, THE FALLOUT AND THE FUTURE

5

THE GOLDEN AGE OF WRESTLING
AND ITS AFTERMATH

With the 1980s came cable television, which allowed previously regional wrestling promoters to show their product across the country. Though it did not initially shake up the territory system, it would by the middle of the decade. According to Jerry Jarrett, Bill Watts approached him because Mid-South Wrestling attendances were down and he wanted to borrow some of Jarrett's talent in hopes of getting his crowds excited again. Jarrett agreed, and in late 1983, a group of wrestlers from the Memphis territory made their way to Mid-South. This group included The Rock 'n' Roll Express, The Midnight Express, along with manager Jim Cornette, Terry Taylor and Bill Dundee, who was brought in to book the territory. Memphis received King Kong Bundy, rookie Rick Rude and Jim "The Anvil" Neidhart. During the Mid-South era (1979–86), nearly every major star in the business passed through the promotion. Stars who made their debuts in the state in this era were former college football player and amateur wrestler "Dr. Death" Steve Williams, Hacksaw Jim Duggan, Magnum T.A., The Road Warriors, Crusher Broomfield / One Man Gang, Butch Reed, Big John Studd, The Mongolian Stomper, Matt Borne, Marty Lunde (Arn Anderson), Ted Allen, Chavo Guerrero, David Sammartino, Larry Zbyszko, Tito Santana, "Mad Dog" Buzz Sawyer, Mil Mascaras, Krusher Darsow, Brad Armstrong, J.J. Dillon, "Leaping" Lanny Poffo, Nikolai Volkoff, Iceman King Parsons, Tom Zenk, The Fantastics, Hercules Hernandez, Shawn Michaels, The Barbarian, Eddie Gilbert, Rob Rechsteiner (Rick Steiner) and The Blade Runners (future superstars Sting

Above: Bill Dundee is one of the most popular wrestlers ever in North Mississippi. He continues to make appearances in the state, although his in-ring career ended in 2019. *Kathy Hinds Moore.*

Opposite: Miriam Springfield. *Carol Springfield Carman.*

and the Ultimate Warrior). NWA World Champion Ric Flair defended his title in the state for the first time in Jackson at the Coliseum on May 4, 1985, against Kerry Von Erich. Flair returned to defend the title in both Jackson and Biloxi in November of that year.

Meanwhile, in Tupelo, the crowds were beginning to shrink. In 1982, Marlin sold his promotional rights for the CWA in Northeast Mississippi to Nettleton drama teacher and playwright turned wrestling superfan Miriam Springfield. Springfield became infatuated with the sport in 1978, when she was invited by her teenage daughter Carol to come with her one Friday night to the weekly Sports Arena shows. Initially, the elder Springfield could not understand her daughter's sudden interest in the sport. Accepting her daughter's invitation, the veteran thespian fell in love with the pageantry and dramatics of the sport. After that night, she not only made it a point to come almost every week to the Tupelo shows, but she also often brought her daughter with her to Saturday morning TV tapings at the Channel 5 studio in Memphis and Monday's big Mid-South Coliseum shows. Along the way, the Springfields became friends with many wrestlers, including "Dirty" Dutch Mantel, the Rock 'n' Roll Express, Bobby Fulton and Terry Taylor. They often cooked breakfast for the wrestlers before Saturday TV tapings, and some of "the boys" affectionately referred to Miriam as "mom."

When the elder Springfield had the opportunity to take her love of wrestling further as a promoter, it was a no-brainer. While the powers that be may have seen the sale as a way to make a quick dollar by selling a sinking ship, the joke was on them. Springfield had the time of her life as a promoter, running Tupelo and towns throughout the northeastern portion of the state. One of the fondest memories of this time for Carol Springfield Carman was when the Fabulous Ones appeared in the 1982 Tupelo Christmas Parade. According to Carol, the flamboyant tag team, decked out in their bow ties and top hats, drove a gold Corvette in the procession with strobe lights flashing and the music of Billy Squier blaring from its radio. By 1983, the Springfield/CWA arrangement had unfortunately ended after attendances had begun to fall further. Instead of being exclusively devoted to Tupelo, Fridays for CWA became spot show days. Among the towns where CWA held occasional shows were Aberdeen, Amory, Booneville, Corinth, Fairview, Fulton, Marks, New Albany, Saltillo and Walnut.

After her run with CWA, Miriam Springfield continued her adventures in wrestling promotion. She partnered with fellow Mississippian Stan "Plowboy" Frazier in a venture called Dixie AllStar Wrestling, running towns like Duck Hill, Mathiston, Moss Point and Philadelphia. The shows featured wrestlers like Junkyard Dog, Memphis-area mainstay Ken Raper, King Cobra and Ed Fluckert. On October 28, 1984, Miriam Springfield passed away at the age of sixty-one from cancer. She was able to enjoy her last several years living a dream she could not have anticipated having just ten years earlier.

Another notable independent company in the 1980s was the Dixie Wrestling Alliance, ran by Tupelo wrestler Floyd Blaylock. The company featured the likes of Aaron and Sammy Holt, The Grave Diggers (Blaylock and partner Greg White), The Interns, Don Bass, Burrhead Jones, Jerry Lantrip, "Dirty" Buddy Ryan, Soulman Hunt, Rocky Lane, Maddog Ewing, Killer Blaylock (not Floyd), Ken "The Dream" Rose, Jimmy Rich, Danny Dodd and Mr. Pro Wrestling. In its initial run, the promotion hosted events at the Louisville Coliseum; National Guard Armories in Eupora, Hattiesburg and Winona; as well as a host of other locales. The company enjoyed a resurgence in the 2000s.

By the early 1980s, territories were beginning to fall, mostly the victims of a second-generation promoter named Vince McMahon Jr. McMahon was not content to remain confined to the Northeast, an area where his father had been tremendously successful for decades. No, McMahon aimed to take his wresting company national and then international. To other promoters, it was clear that McMahon had declared war. With cable television allowing him to bring his gimmick-heavy brand of wrestling to most households across the United States and his presence in the emerging pay-per-view market enabling him to maximize his profits, there was no area of the country where McMahon was unwilling to go. Leading McMahon's charge to take over the wrestling world was the muscled, larger-than-life Hulk Hogan, who had first appeared in Tupelo and Booneville as Terry Boulder for CWA in the late '70s. According to Jerry Jarrett, he gave Hogan the nickname "Hulk" while Hogan was wrestling for him. Besides filling arenas across the country, Hogan's immense popularity allowed the World Wrestling Federation to make millions of dollars in merchandise sales. Besides Hogan, McMahon was able to lure top talent away from other promoters in mass. One of the earliest stars Vince pulled from his competition was Bill Watts's top box-office draw, Junkyard Dog, who left to join the WWF in 1984.

Above: King Cobra is a former USWA Heavyweight Champion, NWA Mid-America Heavyweight Champion and ICW Mississippi Heavyweight and Southern Tag Team Champion. He currently helps train the next generation of stars for Memphis Wrestling. *Tia Howell.*

Left: Dixie Wrestling Alliance advertisement for an event in Yazoo City on Saturday, July 24, 1982. *Jimmy Blaylock.*

Terry Boulder (Hulk Hogan) appearing in Tupelo for CWA. *Kathy Hinds Moore.*

Despite losing its top wrestler, Mid-South still enjoyed relative success in the mid-'80s. In an attempt to appear less regional, Watts dropped "Mid-South" in favor of the bigger-sounding Universal Wrestling Federation (UWF) and began holding events in other areas of the country. Watts was able to get his wrestling program syndicated in dozens of major markets, but this caused him to rack up quite a bill. Because of his aspirations, he began to appear less frequently in his home region, including Mississippi, and attendance for these events began to fall, as jobless rates skyrocketed in the South. As a result, Watts was forced to release several of his top wrestlers. Among the stars he allowed to leave were Hacksaw Jim Duggan, Ted DiBiase, One Man Gang and Butch Reed, all of whom soon ended up in the WWF.

Southern promoters did relatively well against the WWF at first, often outdrawing the northeastern behemoth when running events on the same night in the same general area. However, McMahon's surge was relentless, and on Saturday, October 4, 1986, the World Wrestling Federation held its first event in Mississippi. The event, at Jackson's Mississippi Coliseum, was attended by 4,500 people, about 1,500 more than the UWF shows in the state's capital at that time. The WWF show featured the company's World Heavyweight Champion Hogan versus Hercules Hernandez in the main event, as well as Mississippi's own Kamala against Dick Slater, and Danny Spivey and Mike Rotundo against Greg Valentine and Brutus Beefcake. Koko B. Ware, Hillbilly Jim and others were also on the card. With this one show, it became clear that Mississippi would not be immune to the changes taking place in the national wrestling landscape.

"Tennessee Stud" Ron Fuller decided to expand his Continental Championship Wrestling (CCW) operation into Mississippi in 1986. The third-generation wrestler and promoter had run the company elsewhere in the Southeast since the 1970s. The promotion first entered the state by appearing at Columbus' Lavender Coliseum approximately once a month and in Nanih Waiya, in east-central Mississippi, with similar frequency. Continental's roster included the "Stud" himself; Welch family members

Robert Fuller, Jimmy Golden and Roy Lee Welch (a cousin); and the Armstrong Family, featuring patriarch "Bullet" Bob Armstrong and sons Brad, Scott and Steve. In addition were Tommy Rich, Doug Furnas, Mr. Wrestling II, Jerry Stubbs, Len Denton, "Dirty White Boy" Tony Anthony, Dutch Mantel, "Exotic" Adrian Street, Tom Prichard, the Nightmares, Lord Jonathan Boyd, Mike Golden, "Wildcat" Wendell Cooley, Johnny Rich, Norvell Austin, the New Guinea Headhunters, Frank Lancaster and others. CCW events averaged between 1,000 and 1,500 people in Mississippi, with a few events attracting more or less.

Also in 1986, a new version of Gulf Coast Championship Wrestling was created. The lynchpin and promoter of the new company was "Cowboy" Bob Kelley, arguably the most popular figure in Gulf Coast wrestling history. Joining him were veterans "Hippie" Mike Boyette, Porkchop Cash and "Bruiser" Bob Sweetan, the young team of the Fantastic Ones (Davey Rich and David Baxter), The Bass Brothers, "Marvelous" Marcel Pringle, the masked Blue Yankee, Thomas Tate, Troy Chickaway, Luscious Larry Lane, Red Monroe, Steve Starr, Big Bob Hall, Rick Monroe, Crippler Clark and others. The group ran events at the Wade Kennedy Livestock Arena in Hattiesburg and the North Forrest High School gym in Eatonville,

"Bruiser" Bob Sweetan. *Rex Luther.*

among other places. More independent wrestling companies at this time included the American Wrestling Federation (Louisville area), Southern Championship Wrestling and Confederate States Wrestling (both Eatonville/Forrest County area).

On May 1, 1987, Jim Crockett Promotions (JCP), based in Charlotte, North Carolina, purchased the Universal Wrestling Federation. After the purchase, JCP was in the best position to compete with McMahon's WWF, rivaling it in its number of television markets. Adding to its power, JCP was the home of the charismatic NWA Heavyweight Champion Ric Flair. JCP was unwilling to share him by this point, disregarding the NWA guidelines that had been in place since its founding. They initially attempted to run the UWF and JCP separately, but the two were co-branding events by the end of that year.

With the UWF sold, the Culkins brought Dallas' World Class Championship Wrestling (WCCW) into Jackson and Biloxi a handful of times between March and April 1987 after being asked to do so by Fritz Von Erich, whom George had a previous relationship with from his time wrestling in Texas. This lasted only a few weeks in 1987 but was attempted again in March of the next year, running monthly in a few cities in the state until June. WCCW brought wrestlers to the state like Kerry and Kevin Von Erich, Bruiser Brody, Abdullah the Butcher, The Dingo Warrior (Ultimate Warrior), The Fabulous Freebirds, Terry Taylor, "Gentleman" Chris Adams, The Fantastics, Tony Atlas, Al Madril, Nord the Barbarian, Skip Young, The Samoan Swat Team, The Grappler, "Killer" Tim Brooks Black Bart, Brian Adias, Scott Casey, Vicksburg native Ken Massey, King Cobra, Al Perez, The Missing Link, Wild Bill Irwin, Eric Embry, Solomon Grundy, Jeff Gaylord, Steve Casey, "Hollywood" John Tatum, "midget" wrestlers The Karate Kid and Little Tokyo and managers Percy Pringle III, Gary Hart and General Skandor Akbar.

The World Class shows never really caught on in Mississippi, as evidenced by Leflore County Civic Center manager James Belk's comments in the *Greenwood Commonwealth*. Belk said that wrestling there had gone from 1,500 to 2,000 people attending the events to just 155 for a show in April 1988. He surmised that the massive attendance drop was from the Culkins switching federations. George replied that he thought the main reason was because there were so many wrestling programs on television that many people preferred to stay home and watch.

In the northeastern portion of the state, Jarrett's promotion never really had another long-term weekly town in the state after the early 1980s, but they

Left to right: Bobby Fulton, Lollydude, Tommy Rogers and Kevin Von Erich at Z106 in Jackson, Mississippi, in 1987. *Lolly Griffin.*

still visited the state quite often until the company's end in 1997. Once Watts left Greenwood for the taking, CWA appeared at the Civic Center there from time to time. They also appeared in Charleston and Senatobia with regularity. Some of the wrestlers coming to Mississippi with the company in the late 1980s included the company's kingpin Jerry Lawler and Tommy, Doug and Eddie Gilbert. Also included were manager and Mississippian Downtown Bruno, Jerry Jarrett's son Jeff, Soul Train Jones (Virgil), The Bruise Brothers, Phil Hickerson, a young Scott Steiner, Fabulous Danny Fargo, Don Bass, Big Bubba (Tugboat/Typhoon/Shockmaster), Billy Travis, Miami Vice, Don Bass, Tracey Smothers, manager Missy Hyatt and lady wrestlers Debbie Combs and Despina Montagas.

Jim Crockett Promotions came to the Magnolia State for the first time on April 9, 1987, at Green Coliseum, on the campus of the University of Southern Mississippi. That night's card was headlined by NWA World Heavyweight Champion Ric Flair, defending his title against Nikita Koloff. The show also featured NWA Television Champion Tully Blachard versus Ole Anderson. The event was attended by 2,000 people, a relatively solid number for the company at the time. Two UWF or JCP/UWF co-branded events each also came to Jackson and Biloxi later that year. These cards mostly revolved around UWF talent, though an NWA World Title match was held at one Biloxi event between champion Ric Flair and rival Dusty Rhodes. JCP abandoned the idea of keeping the two entities separate in 1988, and only the Jim Crockett Promotions name survived. In October of that year, the company held events in Jackson and Greenwood. Flair, Rhodes, Lex Luger, Barry Windham, Nikita and Ivan Koloff, Kevin Sullivan and Ron Simmons, as well as former Mid-South stars Dick Murdoch, The Fantastics, The Midnight Express and Eddie Gilbert, were among the bigger stars of these shows. These events were attended by between 1,500 and 2,000 fans. While the company's numbers were good for wrestling of the day, it was a far cry from the number of fans Hulk Hogan had drawn to Jackson a few years earlier. In November 1988, the promotional war between the WWF and JCP intensified when media mogul Ted Turner purchased JCP and renamed it World Championship Wrestling (WCW). The new company began to distance itself from the NWA in the following years and officially left the group in January 1991.

After a successful first trip into Mississippi in 1986, the WWF came back twice to the state capital in 1987. Though neither event featured Hogan, fans did see familiar faces, like Ted DiBiase, Jake "The Snake" Roberts, Kamala, eight-time NWA World Heavyweight Champion Harley Race, Junkyard Dog and One Man Gang. Heavy hitter first appeared during this round of shows, and the shows may have also been the first in Mississippi for "Macho Man" Randy Savage and Bam Bam Bigelow. The event headlined by a WWF World Tag Team Title match featuring the Hart Foundation and the Can-Am Connection (Rick Martel and Tom Zenk) drew 2,081 fans, while the attendance for the later event headlined by a WWF Intercontinental Title match between Honky Tonk Man and Junkyard Dog went unreported. After these two shows, Vince's company seemed to show how insignificant the state was to them, not returning to Mississippi until June 1989.

Backtracking to 1987, an interesting company called World Organization Wrestling (WOW) began appearing in the state. It operated mainly in Alabama, Mississippi and the Pensacola, Florida area. The governing structure of the company was quite complex to understand, even for promoter Rex Luther, who was in charge of the company's Mississippi shows. According to Luther, he paid his booking fees to veteran Mississippi wrestler Rip Tyler, who was the owner of the company as far as outsiders knew. Tyler was being funded by Mr. Ito, a veteran Japanese wrestler who spent much of his career in the southern United States. Ito, according to Luther, was being financed by a Japanese group whose motive in funding the project was not immediately clear. He only recently learned that Ito's motivation was likely to return home to his native Japan and be perceived as a world champion. While WOW was operating in the United States, Ito won the International Championship. When he returned to Japan, he began operating WOW there and sometimes listed himself as "World Champion" on cards. He held the title until his death, after which the title passed to his son.

Luther began working with the company about ten months after it began. At its peak between late 1987 and early 1988, World Organization Wrestling held many shows around the Mississippi Delta, including events in Clarksdale, Cleveland, Greenwood and Greenville. Other towns the promotion visited included Louisville, Lucedale, Philadelphia and Yazoo City. For a short time, the company had a television program on WXVT 15 in Greenville, though most of the episodes would never be aired throughout the United States.

The company featured future stars like Giant Kokina (Yokozuna), Big Bubba and Bob Holly in some of their earlier outings. Joining these soon-to-be major stars were veteran regional workers like Bob Sweetan, Mr. Olympia, David Haskins, Scott Armstrong and tag teams Bad Company, The Batten Twins and The New Fabulous Fargos, managed by veteran Don Fargo. There was also "Marvelous" Marcel Pringle, Ron Starr and Ted Oates. Lesser-known talents like Montgomery County deputy and wrestler Tank Davis, Shawn Baxter, Rex Rodgers (billed at seven feet, two inches tall), Hacksaw Higgins, Huggie Bear Brown, Superstar Chris Allen and "midget" wrestlers Macho Midget and Little John were also on the roster. In 1988, Tyler informed Luther that his funding was beginning to dry up, so he began cutting down on Mississippi dates before ending them altogether. The company was abandoned for the most part in the United States, although Luther says that he received calls from the group through the mid-1990s asking him to send them television programs. At these times, he usually filmed matches in Sharkey County with stars like Junkyard Dog and Brickhouse Brown, along with a host of local wrestlers.

Another independent promotion was a company that called itself Mid-South Championship Wrestling, which operated around the summer of 1987 and ran the Louisville and Kosciusko Coliseums. This would be one of several variants of the Mid-South Wrestling name that would appear in the late 1980s and the 1990s. It featured the Scuffling Hillbillies (Uncle Elmer and Cousin Junior), The Bruise Brothers, The Southland Express and The River City Bombers: David Price (Motley Cruz) and Van Van Horne. There was also The Masked Medics, Man Mountain Link, Odyssey, Chris

Left: Bob Holly applies a rear chin lock to Mr. Olympia at a WOW event. *Rex Luther*.

Right: A veteran Motley Cruz, along with manager "Hollywood" Jimmy Blaylock, appears at an OWO wrestling event in Amory on February 25, 2017. *Tia Howell*.

Frazier, veteran "Dandy" Jack Donovan, Bo Sullivan and Tony Miles. Other independent promotions operating at the time were the Southern Wrestling Federation (featuring Mike Rose and other local wrestlers) and the National Wrestling Federation (featuring Don Bass, Davey Rich, Bobo Reed, Steve Starr and other locals).

Gorgeous Ladies of Wrestling (GLOW) made appearances in the Magnolia State in 1988 in Biloxi and Philadelphia. The all-female promotion had a syndicated television show, which appeared on WXXV in Gulfport, among other stations throughout the state and country. Some of the stars of the organization included Tina Ferrari (Ivory), Mountain Fiji, the Farmer's Daughters and Ninotchka. This company was the inspiration for the Netflix series of the same name that premiered in 2017.

By September 1988, the Culkins switched promotions again and began bringing in the recently renamed Continental Wrestling Federation (CWF). Ron Fuller sold the company, originally named Continental Championship Wrestling, to Alabama television magnate David Woods in late 1987. Woods brought in Eddie Gilbert and Paul E. Dangerously to book the promotion. Another familiar face, Jack Curtis Jr., George's nephew, served as the on-screen commissioner. The Culkin-promoted Continental shows ran mostly in Biloxi, joining towns that Continental already visited like Ackerman, Calhoun City, Carrolton, Columbus, Kosciusko, Louisville and Meridian. Lord Humongous (Sid Vicious), Shane Douglas, Tony Anthony, Willie B. Hert ("Pistol" Pez Whatley), Detroit Demolition, (Randy Colley / Moondog Rex), Nightmare Freddy (Doug Gilbert), The Samoan Warriors (Sika and Kokina) and The Japanese Connection (Mr. [Masa] Chono and RPM) were some of the additions who visited Mississippi with the CWF in those days.. Even though the company had a slot on cable television's Financial News Network, Woods's time in pro wrestling was ultimately unsuccessful, and CWF closed in late 1989.

In February 1989, WCCW, on its deathbed, came back into Biloxi and Greenwood for one last try. In addition to the normal WCCW crew, future stars Super Black Ninja (Great Muta) and Cactus Jack Manson made these trips. This run lasted for just a handful of shows, signaling the Culkins' exit from the wrestling business. Their contributions to the state's wrestling history are indelible, and no in-state promoter has been able to come close to the level of success they achieved at their peak.

Later in 1989, Jerry Jarrett purchased the ailing World Class Championship Wrestling and merged it with CWA to form the United States Wrestling Association (USWA). The new company briefly ran events in Texas, but it mainly stayed in Tennessee, Kentucky and North Mississippi. The company frequently appeared at Clarksdale's City Auditorium and in towns like Oxford. USWA stars of the early '90s were veterans like Jerry Lawler, Bill Dundee, Tommy Rich, Eddie Gilbert, the Moondogs and Billy Jack Haynes, and younger talents like Jeff Jarrett, Lawler's son Brian Christopher, Doug Gilbert, PG-13 (Wolfie D and J.C. Ice [Dundee's son]), Reggie B. Fine, Flash Flanagan, Brian Lee, Rex King, Steven Dunn and female wrestler Miss Texas.

The WWF returned to Biloxi and Jackson in 1989. The next year, it made three appearances in Biloxi, drawing 3,100 fans at one of the shows, as well as one show in Jackson, which drew 6,000 people. The Jackson show featured Ted DiBiase versus Big Boss Man and, in another contest at the top of the card, the Ultimate Warrior and "The Texas Tornado" Kerry Von Erich against Mr. Perfect and Rick Rude. Other notables that night were tag team champions Demolition, The Hart Foundation and Dusty Rhodes's son Dustin in his first year. The Biloxi shows include many of the same stars, as well as former NWA lynchpin Dusty Rhodes, Randy Savage, Tito Santana, Jake Roberts, Akeem (One Man Gang), manager

Grandmaster Sexay (Brian Christopher) appears at SWA Wrestling in Southaven, Mississippi, on January 19, 2018. *Tia Howell.*

Bobby Heenan, Earthquake, Tugboat, Sgt. Slaughter and the popular young tag team The Rockers.

In 1991, the WWF appeared twice in Biloxi, one event being a television taping for *WWF Wrestling Challenge*. The taping drew 9,176 people. Because it was a television event, most matches were "squash" matches, or one-sided matches featuring a wrestler the company was trying to make look good against a jobber, or wrestler whose only purpose was to make his opponent look good. The exception was a WWF World Title match between champion Hogan and challenger Sgt. Slaughter. DiBiase, Big Boss Man, The Legion of Doom, Earthquake, the new WWF phenom The Undertaker and others were on this big show. In 1992, Biloxi held another television taping, though this was the company's only visit to the state that year. It was evidently not as successful, as attendance figures for that night were not made public. The card featured a tag team match pitting Hogan and Roddy Piper against the recently arrived Ric Flair and Sid Justice, as well as Savage against Roberts and Shawn Michaels versus Piper. In addition, there were appearances from The Undertaker, The Nasty Boys, the British Bulldog, Papa Shango, Bret Hart and The Natural Disasters, among others. At this time, the WWF was definitely number one in the state, but WCW showed no signs of giving up.

With Ted Turner's money ensuring that it could stay in the battle for the long run, WCW made Mississippi a priority, appearing seven times in the Magnolia State between 1989 and 1991. The company appeared not only in the WWF-frequented areas of Biloxi and Jackson, but also in Greenwood and Meridian. While in Jackson, it held a taping for its *NWA World Wide Wrestling* television program and another for its *NWA Power Hour* and *NWA Main Event* programs in Greenwood. The main stars on these WCW shows were Ric Flair, emerging star Sting, Lex Luger, Arn Anderson, Sid Vicious, The Road Warriors, The Steiner Brothers, Doom, Brian Pillman, Barry Windham, Bam Bam Bigelow and Cactus Jack. There were also stars past their prime, like Junkyard Dog, Harley Race and The Iron Sheik. Perhaps because of low attendance, the company did not visit the state in 1992. Reported attendance for these shows generally ranged between two thousand and three thousand, but one Jackson event in 1990 drew a disappointing four hundred people, and the attendance for several of them were not made public.

When the Culkins left the wrestling business, an assortment of promoters attempted to fill the void in the state. Many of these promoters came to Gil Culkin for advice at the time. He cautioned them, "If there was money left to be made, do you think we would have left?" However, the fall of the territory system left a lot of big-name talent that was not under contract with

Sting was WCW's most steady force in the 1990s. Besides WCW, he wrestled in the state for UWF and TNA. *Wikimedia Commons.*

WWF or WCW, and promoters and many fans were itching to have regular wrestling matches back in the state. Some of the bigger names to work multiple Mississippi independent promotions in the 1990s were Junkyard Dog, "Dr. Death" Steve Williams, Sid Vicious, Abdullah the Butcher, The Rock 'n' Roll Express, Butch Reed, The Fantastics, "Nature Boy" Buddy Landell, Kamala, Terry Taylor, Terry Gordy, One Man Gang, Bob Orton Jr., Greg Valentine, Koko B. Ware, Eddie and Doug Gilbert, Bill Dundee, Jimmy Valiant, Mabel, The Armstrongs, one version or another of Doink The Clown, Tracey Smothers, Adrian Street, "Wildcat" Wendell Cooley, Cora and Debbie Combs, The New Spoiler, Ron and Don Bass, Mr. Olympia, Cousin Luke (Gene Lewis), David Haskins (Davey Rich), Reggie B. Fine, King Cobra, Mr. Wrestling III and Brickhouse Brown. Also included was the ladies feud that traveled for over a decade, Bambi versus Peggy Lee Leather. Local and regional talent frequently appearing on independent shows around the state included workers like Brother Heaven Lee Love, Kenny Valiant, "Hot Shot" Cassidy O'Reilly, Lord Humongous (Gary Nations), "Mr. Nasty" Ken Massey, Babaraz, The Jagged Edge, Cedric Crain, Michael Darkhart, Johnny Reb, Rude Dog, Thomas Tate, manager "Hollywood" Jimmy Blaylock, Rainbow Brown, Joe Kane, Primetime Jimmy Valentine, Max Pain, "Outlaw" J.D. McKay, Steve Starr, Calvin Rose, Atomic Dog, Danny B. Goode, Sammy Hall, Mr. Bojangles, Tojo Yamamoto Jr., Hurricane Bronson, Stan Sweetan, David Hart, Viper, The Southern Express and lady wrestlers Robin Southern and Lady Elvira.

The Culkins sold a wrestling ring and other tools of the trade to an ambitious young promoter named Thomas C. Parker, who first worked with Heritage Championship Wrestling (HCW) in October 1989 and booked events in towns like Vicksburg and Clarksdale. His shows, which he booked with help from territory veteran Buck Robley, featured a host of talented wrestlers. It was one of the earliest places where young, second-generation star Dustin Rhodes wrestled. Unfortunately, Heritage lasted only four

Bambi saves Lollydude from the clutches of "Mr. Nasty" Ken Massey while referee Keith Lansdale is tied up in the corner with Peggy Lee Leather. This photo was taken in 1991 at the Central Mississippi State Fair in Kosciusko. *Lolly Griffin.*

months. Commenting on the final days of HCW via the Wrestlingclassics. com message board in 2010, Parker wrote, "I just burned through my money before the tv had time to get over." After HCW, Parker became the Mississippi promoter for a company called Five Star Wrestling (FSW) run by Grizzly Smith, Jack Curtis Jr. and Louisiana promoter Jimmy Kilshaw. FSW had much of the same talent as Heritage, but it spotlighted Smith's children Sam Houston and Rockin' Robin. Before Parker could get much work done with Five Star Wrestling, he was stopped in his tracks.

Around this time, Parker began to develop a bad reputation with many wrestlers and fellow promoters. Parker even pled guilty to federal fraud charges stemming from his early time in the business. In 2012, via the same message board referenced in the previous paragraph, Parker described the time he ran HCW as "Crazy but fun times—but so rough when it ended." In 2005, he created IPWA Wrestling, which included many of the bigger names in the area as well as lesser-known guys like AXL Ozz and Steve Southern.

Parker ran the promotion until 2006, publishing his decision to close it in an ad in the *Clarion-Ledger*. In it, he writes, "[The wrestling business] has brought me far more pain (than fond memories)." In a portion of the note written to his wife, he begs her forgiveness for what he called his "selfish desires for success."

Of course, Parker's time in the wrestling business did not end with his public declaration. In the late 2000s, he began working for Traditional Championship Wrestling, a well-received Arkansas-based independent promotion. He even had an on-screen role there. His time there seemed good for everyone, though the company folded in 2014. Fast-forward to 2021, when Parker revived Heritage Wrestling for an event he called the Inaugural Brawl. The *Vicksburg Daily News* reported that wrestlers who participated in the event claimed they were never paid after having to help set up the ring and wrestling twice that night. When I reached out to Mr. Parker to discuss his time in the wrestling business, I was told: "Maybe some time in the future. I am busy this weekend." That time has yet to come.

Then there was Lollydude, the persona of Lolly Griffin from Bunkie, Louisiana. He got into wrestling after meeting and befriending many of the stars of Mid-South Wrestling while living in Alexandria, Louisiana, and working as a disc jockey. Lolly oozes the charisma needed to excel in the hyperbolic radio and wrestling worlds. He attributes most of his in-ring training to Vicksburg wrestling veteran Ken Massey. Besides wrestling himself, Lolly also got into the promotional end of the business, which made great use of his skill set. His first endeavor in Mississippi wrestling was called the Mid-South Wrestling Federation (MSWF). It ran between 1991 and 1992. The company worked all over Mississippi and Louisiana and featured many wrestlers common to the state, as well as former World Class Wrestling talents like "Gentleman" Chris Adams, manager Skandor Akbar, Bill Irwin, Black Bart, Iceman King Parsons and "Crazy" Mike Davis. Griffin said the company had a solid setup, with television deals in Mississippi, Louisiana and parts of Arkansas. According to him, the promotion ended when the Texas investor was found to be a fake and went to prison for writing a slew of fraudulent checks.

A few years after the demise of MSWF, Lolly formed a friendship with Jackson's WBDB Fox 40 general manager Al Tanksley and his family after they worked together for a few Children's Miracle Network telethons. The station was interested in producing its own wrestling show and wanted Griffin to help them run it. With that, Deep South Wrestling (DSW) was born. Griffin says that this program was also sold to markets throughout

MSWF poster from a Kosciusko event. *Lolly Griffin.*

Left to right: Gene "Cousin Luke" Lewis, James "Kamala" Harris (without makeup) and Lollydude. *Lolly Griffin.*

Mississippi and Louisiana, as well as parts of Alabama. DSW began in January 1995, with its television tapings taking place at the new Silver Star Casino in Philadelphia. Hercules, Disco Inferno, Dick Murdoch, Demolition Ax, Johnny Mantell and Erik Watts were a few of the new faces that popped up in DSW. Vicksburg native Jack Curtis Jr. served in the role of on-screen commissioner. Unfortunately, two factors led to the demise of the promising company before its first year was over. First, DSW's contract with the Silver Star Casino wasn't renewed, because several drunken wrestlers had created problems while staying at the casino hotel. Second, according to Griffin, he was ousted from the company when it believed it could make the product without him. This led to a mass exodus from the company, including stars like Terry Taylor and Gene Lewis, who had major roles in DSW.

Griffin's third and final wrestling promotion in Mississippi was called Southern Championship Wrestling (SCW). This company began in 1996 and was arguably Griffin's most successful. SCW had a large television reach, and the ratings for the show were quite good. Prior to the founding of the promotion, Griffin met aspiring wrestlers "Hot Shot" Cassidy O'Reilly and Cedric "Ced-Man" Crain. The company served as a launching pad for their careers, which ended up being relatively successful. Crain was also instrumental in lining up financing for the endeavor. Besides the two rookies and many Mid-South veterans, David Haskins and his newest trainee, former Philadelphia High School and Oklahoma Sooner football sensation and ex-NFL player Marcus Dupree, notably appeared in the promotion. Jack Curtis Jr. was again brought in, this time to form a three-man announcing team with Lollydude and Bob Morris. The promotion ran for two years, but it could have likely gone much longer had the promotion's financier not faced federal charges himself for illegal activities involving the video poker business he was running at the time. All of his business affairs were frozen, ending the company, as its operating capital was granted on an as-needed basis. After this third attempt failed, Griffin distanced himself from promoting wrestling and concentrated on other adventures befitting one called Lollydude.

Going back to Marcus Dupree, he grew up a wrestling fan, particularly enjoying the work of Junkyard Dog and Jerry Lawler. While playing football at Oklahoma, Dupree was teammates and friends with Steve Williams, who became involved with professional wrestling even before his college career was completed. "Dr. Death" encouraged him to consider pro wrestling after his football career ended. It was wrestler Steve Armstrong who led Dupree to David Haskins (Rich), who had several ties to the Magnolia State himself. It was 1995, and Dupree was staying in Memphis' Peabody Hotel while playing football for the Arena Football League's Memphis Pharaohs when he and Haskins first met. Haskins invited Dupree to come live with him and train, which Dupree accepted. He began wrestling in USWA that year, teaming with Haskins in a feud with Jack Hammer and Crusher Bones. According to Dupree, he worked there for about six months before deciding that he did not want to pursue the sport for the long term. He made this decision when he learned of the WWF's rigorous schedule and decided it was not something he aspired to do. After his USWA run, Dupree continued to wrestle throughout the South on occasion. While working for SCW, Dupree also had the opportunity to team up with his old pal Steve Williams.

Another notable promoter who started in the early '90s was John Horton. Horton was trained in the ring by his cousin Don Jardine (The Spoiler) and veteran Oni Wiki Wiki. He initially wrestled as The Magician before adopting the persona of the masked Dr. X. Horton started his own promotion, Pro Wrestling International, in 1991 because of his disdain for the cartoonish nature of popular wrestling at the time. He soon changed his promotion's name to Mid-South Championship Wrestling and enjoyed a long, successful run, operating until 2005. Horton's brand of wrestling involved less talk and more in-ring action, and his events were free of wrestlers with over-the-top gimmicks. Even though Vince McMahon had publicly admitted that wrestling contests were scripted in the late 1980s, Horton says that he thinks that 70 percent of his audience believed his shows were real, due to his company's style. In 1994, the company produced an excellent television product that featured "Nightmare" Ted Allen and Cactus Jack as announcers and Mark Curtis as referee. Unfortunately,

Dr. X (John Horton) and "Nature Boy" Buddy Landell. *John Horton.*

The Jagged Edge, the last ever North American Heavyweight Champion for Horton. *John Horton.*

Bert Prentice as Christopher Love for Gulf Coast Championship Wrestling. *Rex Luther.*

the show's production limited Horton's family time too much, so he discontinued it. Of note, Stan Hansen, who lived in Jackson for many years, and Unabomb (a young and inexperienced Kane) appeared in his promotion. Horton also feels pride in having trained Mississippi independent stars Brother Heaven Lee Love, The Jagged Edge and Babaraz. "They kept wrestling alive in Mississippi for a decade," Horton said of the trio.

After World Organization Wrestling, promoter Rex Luther began working for Crusher Blackwell's Southern Wrestling in Georgia. He helped sell advertising and brought in Mississippi grapplers like Tank Davis, Bobo Reed and Chris Allen to wrestle there. A few months later, he came back to Mississippi and teamed with Tennessee's Bert Prentice to form another incarnation of Gulf Coast Championship Wrestling. Despite its name, this company spent most of its time running the Clarksdale and Jackson areas. The company saw great crowds in Clarskdale for a company its size, with one show drawing over 2,500 people. Prentice worked as manager/wrestler Christopher Love, and stars like Junkyard Dog and Ivan Koloff made appearances for the group. Luther's and Prentice's trainees, like Mark Terranova and several masked wrestlers, filled out the rest of the shows.

Wrestling fan Bill Bailey promoted the National Wrestling Federation (NWF), yet another company trying to take its product national, around Hattiesburg and Ellisville between 1989 and 1990. This company, based in the northeastern United States, was owned by Bob Raskin. Unfortunately for Raskin, he did not have the resources to compete with WWF and WCW. Some of the wrestlers who appeared for the NWF were Wendi

Richter, Sheik El Shaad, veteran Tom Jones, The Masked Executioners, the USA Express and Bob "The Gambler" Owens. Another company that came through Mississippi once was Afa Anoa'i's Trans World Wrestling Federation (TWWF). It came to Mississippi Delta Community College's J.T. Hall Coliseum in Moorhead on December 13, 1990. This trip was likely taken to see Afa's nephew Matt Anoa'i (future Rosey/Kimo in WWE), who was playing football at the community college. Matt's father, Sika, his cousin The Great Kokina and Mid-South regulars like The Batten Twins, Taurus Bulba (Bruiser Bedlam) and Jimmy Jack Funk were all on the card that night.

According to Doug McKay, a mother-daughter duo from Alabama briefly ran shows in Greenwood and Louisville in February 1990. The main stars of the shows were Continental alumni like Dr. Tom Pritchard, Wendell Cooley, Frankie Lancaster and Ron Harris, as well as the New York Brawler (Lou Fabiano), Mark White and others. In May of that year, Northwest Championship Wrestling, operated by Alabama promoter Eddy Forsyth, ran shows in the area. The shows featured the likes of Tracey Youngblood, The Moondog, The Stormtroopers, The Cruiser, Atomic Dog, Ebony Price, Michael Money, The Hollywood Blonde, The Southern Rocker and The Rockin' Rebels.

In the northeast portion of the state, wrestlers like Aaron Holt, Sammy Hall, Dennis Upton and Kenny Valiant who had trained in Tupelo at its 1970s peak promoted the sport in the late '80s and '90s. Valiant's company, All-Pro Championship Wrestling (APCW), operated throughout Mississippi until the early 2010s, booking towns all over the state, including Batesville, Bruce, Carthage and countless others. The events featured a mix of bigger names like Jimmy Valiant, Jerry Lawler, Bill Dundee and Kamala with local talent. At one point, longtime Crenshaw mayor Oscar Barlow served as an announcer for APCW. Barlow is a lifelong wrestling fan and a great ambassador for the sport in Mississippi. He continues to make sporadic appearances around the northern portion of the state. Sammy Hall's company, Bad Boys Promotions Wrestling, operated until his death in 2014, holding events from Kosciusko to Saltillo. Tennessee-born wrestling brothers Lee and Billy Ray Hickerson also promoted shows in Corinth around this time. Wrestlers in this part of the state included Bad Boy Burns, Big Bubba Humphries, Bruise Brother Bruno, Thomas Jannetty, The Mississippi Blondes (Charlie Boo and Greg Hawkes), "Rockin'" Rick Jackson, Jimmy Rich, Benny Traylor, Doc Rose, ladies Maniac Monica and Dixieland Delight and others.

Left: Wrestling announcer and former multiterm mayor of Crenshaw, Oscar Barlow. *Kenny Valiant*.

Below: "Showtime" Willie Valiant, Ken "The Dream" Rose and "Handsome" Jimmy Valiant pose for a picture in Pontotoc, Mississippi. This was the night before Rose became "Luscious" Kenny Valiant. *Kenny Valiant*.

"Luscious" Kenny Valiant and longtime heel manager "Hollywood" Jimmy Blaylock had been friends since they attended Tupelo High School together, often spending weekends at each other's houses watching wrestling. In 1991, Valiant asked Blaylock to come manage him at a show in Fulton, because he thought it would take Blaylock's mind off of some recent hardships. That night, Blaylock found that he excelled at infuriating the crowd, and he also loved it. He has now started on his fourth decade in the business. Also in 1991, "Handsome" Jimmy Valiant invited the former Ken "The Dream" Rose into his extended wrestling family after years of battles between the two, an honor that Kenny continues to take pride in.

Around 1992, Laurel-area wrestler Eddie "Hot Stuff" Breland operated Mid-American Championship Wrestling around towns in South Mississippi like Seminary and Wiggins. Among the wrestlers who worked for Breland were The Mercenaries, Monster Murdock, King Mohammed, Desperado, Joey "The Body" Barrett, Headhunter, County Mountie and Hollywood Rusty. Another regional company that toured Mississippi in the latter half of 1992 was South-Atlantic Professional Wrestling, which was being run by Paul Jones and Frank Dusek. The Carolina-based company came through Liberty, McComb and Brookhaven and featured P.N. News, "Pistol" Pez Whatley, a young Rob Van Dam, The Nightstalker (Bryan Clarke), Scott Studd (Riggs) and others.

By mid-1993, the WWF was undergoing major changes. Hulk Hogan was gone from the company, as were veteran stars like the Ultimate Warrior, Jake Roberts and Hacksaw Jim Duggan. The company would lose some steam during this time, particularly in the South. They appeared in Biloxi once in 1993, featuring the Undertaker in the main event against an inexperienced, legitimate giant, Giant Gonzalez. The card, which featured Bret Hart, Lex Luger, Kamala, Tito Santana and a host of younger talent, drew a lackluster 2,200 people. The WWF would not book the state at all in 1994 before deciding to try its luck in the northern cities of Tupelo and Robinsonville in 1995. Both shows drew 2,000 or less. The 1995 North Mississippi shows were headlined

Ken "The Dream" Rose shakes hands with Sammy Hall. *Kenny Valiant.*

by WCW castoff Razor Ramon against WWF veteran Bob Backlund. Also on the cards were the British Bulldog, Mid-South veteran King Kong Bundy, Tatanka, Mabel, The Smoking Gunns, Man Mountain Rock and others.

During WWF's transition period, WCW made Mississippi a greater priority and gained momentum there. In 1993 alone, it visited the state at least five times. It hit up former wrestling hotbeds Clarksdale and Louisville and visited the often-overlooked coastal city of Pascagoula. Most notable of all, the company brought its *Beach Blast* pay-per-view show to Biloxi at the Mississippi Coast Coliseum, placing the most importance on the state it had seen since the late 1970s. The non-televised events did not have great numbers, but *Beach Blast* was attended by between 7,000 and 8,600 people, although how much of that came from actual ticket sales is uncertain. The event is remembered more for its silly, elaborate promotional trailer than anything that happened inside the ring, but it wasn't a terrible event. A tag team match pitting Sting and the British Bulldog against the Masters of the Powerbomb (Sid Vicious and Big Van Vader) headlined the event. Other notable names on the card included the returning Ric Flair, Barry Windham, Brian Pillman, Arn Anderson, a young "Stunning" Steve Austin, Dustin Rhodes, Lord Steven Regal and former WWF and territory star Rick Rude.

As it became legal to operate casinos in the state, many of the gaming establishments began looking for entertainment to draw crowds. Casinos and wrestling seemed like a natural marriage. Other states had shown that these partnerships could be advantageous for both parties. The first notable casino wrestling show happened in April 1993 at the Splash Casino in Tunica. The "Clash at the Splash" featured veteran Honky Tonk Man. Casinos continue to hold wrestling events today, particularly at Lula's Isle of Capri.

WCW continued its press on the state in 1994, appearing three times in Tupelo that year. Each show drew between two thousand and three thousand people, showing that many fans in Northeast Mississippi were ready to see big-time wrestling once again. WCW also appeared twice in Bay St. Louis' Casino Magic. Though Hulk Hogan arrived in the company in the summer of 1994, he did not appear on any of these Mississippi shows. Instead, they featured a mix of WCW mainstays like Sting, Ric Flair, Vader and Harlem Heat and recently arrived veterans like Hacksaw Jim Duggan, Guardian Angel (Big Bossman) and Honky Tonk Man.

In 1995, WCW hosted its first of three pay-per-view shows in the city of Tupelo. According to Eric Bischoff, who ran the company at the time, WCW booked so many high-profile events in the city because of its proximity to

The Barbarian was a member of the Alliance to End Hulkamania in the main event of *WCW Uncensored 1996*. Here he is on Sunday, March 8, 2015, for CWA Wrestling in Ripley, Mississippi, against Danny Dollar. *Tia Howell.*

the company's Atlanta headquarters. WCW's first pay-per-view event in the All-America City, *Uncensored 1995*, is remembered as one of the worst in the company's history. In the main event of the first *Uncensored*, champion Hulk Hogan somehow won a strap match over Vader by dragging Ric Flair (who was dressed in drag) to all four corners of the ring. The event is also remembered for the debut of the Renegade. Leading up to the event, WCW had been strongly hinting at the appearance of the Ultimate Warrior. Instead, what they delivered was an independent wrestler doing his best Warrior impersonation, much to the chagrin of the audiences in the arena and at home. The night also featured several gimmick matches, including a boxer versus wrestler match, a lights-out match, a martial-arts match, an unsuccessful attempt to re-create the famous Tupelo Concession Stand Brawl and an infamous "King of the Road" match that led to the firings of Dustin Rhodes and Barry Darsow (working as the Blacktop Bully). The two were terminated for bleeding during the match, which was against company policy at the time. The match, which took place in the back of an eighteen-wheeler, was actually filmed days earlier near Atlanta and shown at the event. The attendance for *Uncensored 95* was 5,782, a decent number at the time for a pay-per-view show of little consequence.

The event returned in 1996, drawing a large attendance of around nine thousand people, which signaled an upswing for WCW and professional wrestling as a whole. While the card was better in most areas, the main event Doomsday Cage Match was worse than anything the previous year. It featured top faces Hulk Hogan and Randy Savage taking on eight men, collectively known as the Alliance to End Hulkamania. The group included Ric Flair, Lex Luger, Arn Anderson, Kevin Sullivan, Meng, The Barbarian, Z-Gangsta and The Ultimate Solution. The three-layered cage was positioned beside the entryway, a hard position for most of the live audience to see. Despite the main event's failure, the card featured excellent matches between the newly arrived Konnan and Eddie Guererro and another great contest between Lord Steven Regal and the Belfast Bruiser (Fit Finlay), as well as some other decent matches.

6

A NEW ATTITUDE

I n the summer of 1996, The New World Order (NWO) took the wrestling world hostage. The stable featured a heel Hulk Hogan (Hollywood Hogan) and recent WWF headliners Scott Hall and Kevin Nash. With the arrival of the NWO, wrestling was becoming less cartoonish and more reality based. Nash and Hall headlined WCW's next Tupelo show, a non-televised event in October 1996. Harlem Heat, Sting, Randy Savage, The Giant (Big Show), "Diamond" Dallas Page, Eddie Guerrero and Chris Jericho were also on the card, which drew 3,000 fans. In April 1997, WCW returned to Tupelo for a third pay-per-view event. *Spring Stampede 1997* was an okay show, and the main event between "Macho Man" Randy Savage and "Diamond" Dallas Page received high praise. The event drew 8,356 people, which is relatively good considering the absence of Hogan, Sting and Flair on the show. Joining the usual WCW crew on the card were rising stars like Chris Benoit, Dean Malenko and Rey Mysterio Jr.

WWF was on the verge of its breakout Attitude era when it returned to the state and brought its flagship *Raw Is War* program into Biloxi on August 11, 1997, after a more than two-year hiatus. The episode featured longtime WWF stars like The Undertaker, Shawn Michaels, Bret Hart and Owen Hart, as well as repackaged guys like Mankind (Cactus Jack), Goldust (Dustin Rhodes) and Farooq (Ron Simmons). Memphis megastar and WWF commentator and occasional wrestler Jerry Lawler and his son, USWA star Brian Christopher, were also on the card that night. Arguably the two biggest stars of the Attitude era, "Stone Cold" Steve Austin and The Rock, did not wrestle on this card, which drew 6,814.

Just two months later, WCW's competing program, *Monday Nitro*, visited the same arena, drawing only 5,950 fans. This suggests that, perhaps, the WWF had regained its grip on the Mississippi Gulf Coast. WCW's show featured its usual cast of characters, plus a future superstar named Bill Goldberg, WWF veteran Curt Hennig and others. Between 1998 and 1999, when the company reached its peak and began its descent, WCW made nine appearances in the state, including three each in Biloxi, Jackson and Tupelo. One of the Biloxi stops was to film another *Monday Nitro* episode. In 1998, when the company was still on top, events in the state averaged between 7,000 and 9,000 people. By the next year, that average had fallen to between 3,500 and 5,000. The exception to this was the Biloxi *Nitro*, which outperformed WCW's and WWF's previous outings at around 9,000 people. Except for Goldberg's emergence as a main eventer and longtime WWF star Bret Hart's defection to WCW, the roster looked much the same as it had in earlier years.

Going back to the indies, the Southeast Wrestling Federation, which wrestler Big Don Brodie ran weekly in Charleston, burst onto the scene in 1995. T.L. Cruze, Tommy Lane, The Grim Reaper, Stacy Awesome and others were a part of the promotion. Around 1997, two devoted wrestling fans, Billy McClain and Jim Griffin, created an independent wrestling variety show called *South's Greatest Wrestling Fans* that first aired on a local, low-power station. The show included footage shot at area independent events, like Brodie's, as well as some from around the United States and Canada. The show was successful and syndicated in a handful of markets in the South, thanks to help from NWA Wildside owner Bill Behrens. When McClain decided to try his hand at promoting shows, Behrens provided him with guidance and the talent for his initial events. He also encouraged McClain to join the National Wrestling Alliance, which still existed, though it lacked the power it had over the sport decades earlier. The alliance allowed independent promoters across the country to share resources, talent and collective championships. When McClain joined the collective in 1999, NWA Mississippi was born. One of its earliest stars was Big Don Brodie, who held the NWA National Heavyweight Title twice between 2000 and 2001. Another major player was Yazoo City's Brother Heaven Lee Love, who became the first NWA Mississippi Junior Heavyweight Champion and eventually bought into the company. He served as head trainer for the company's wrestling school. In 2002, McClain moved south and relocated his promotion to a small building in Magee, rebranding it NWA Battlezone.

Brother Heaven Lee Love flexes for opponent and former WCW/WWE star Buff Bagwell, while veteran wrestler J.D. McKay, serving as the referee, looks on. *Tia Blaylock.*

NWA Battlezone was the steadiest independent wrestling presence in the state until McClain sold the promotion in 2012. The company is still in operation though no longer affiliated with NWA. Some of the wrestlers who have appeared with the company in its long run include Hacksaw Jim Duggan, Chris Champion, Porkchop Cash, The Colorado Kid, Rodney Mack, Steven Dunn, Reno Riggins, Ricky Murdoch, Lance Jade, Blade Boudreaux, The Sniper, Chris Anthony, Todd Morton, The Patriot, Austin Rhodes, Joey Venture, Denny Cooley, Scott Storm, Bill Hanson, David Young, Rip Steele, A.C. Brown, Joey C, Sirus Levay, Sean O'Reilly, Jesse Dalton, Cody Mantell, Mike Carter, Psycho Faroh of Funk, Cale Connors, Eric Black, Frankie Williamson, Nick Wonder, Damien Storm, Chris Black, Wesley Jenkins, Pat Patera and others. In 2003, promoter and wrestler Bob Serio began operating NWA New South, an affiliate promotion of NWA Mississippi (Battlezone). The company ran shows around the Delta area for about five years.

In the late 1990s and early 2000s, when wrestling was booming, town festivals in several parts of the state were itching to have wrestling on their schedule. McClain's promotion was a part of Greenville's and Greenwood's Balloon Fests and Raleigh's Bayfest. Greenwood's 1999 Balloon Fest drew an impressive two thousand fans for its wrestling event. The 1999 High Cotton Cooking Contest in Greenwood featured matches from Dwayne Huckaba and Chris Rose's American Championship Wrestling, while Clarksdale preferred to outsource its sports entertainment to St. Louis promoter Henry Hubbard's International Championship Wrestling between 1998 and 2000.

Another of the bigger independents at the time was the Yazoo City–based International Wrestling Federation (IWF), owned by local businessman Guy Walters. The company brought a variety of popular veterans and younger local stars into the area, like former WCW and territory star Bunkhouse

Back row, left to right: Kenny Valiant, Michael Darkheart, Buddy Landell and Tracy Smothers. *Second row, left to right*: referee Willie D. Charisma, Don Bass, Ricky Morton and Babaraz. *Front row, left to right*: Robert Gibson and The Jagged Edge. *Kenny Valiant.*

Buck (Jimmy Golden), local Playboy Mike Rhodes and many others. On June 1, 1998, veteran Junkyard Dog was driving back to Mississippi to work on an IWF show after spending the weekend attending his daughter's high school graduation in North Carolina. In Lake, Mississippi, eight miles outside Forest, the forty-five-year-old was killed in an automobile accident. It is a bit poetic, though no less tragic, that the biggest performer in the history of the Mid-South Wrestling territory lost his life traveling the same roads he did during his prime.

In the Gulfport area, King Style Wrestling was a small company and school that operated from at least 1996 to around 2001. Ken and Bobbie Jefcoat owned the organization, where Ken wrestled as "The Fabulous Godfather." Other wrestlers for the group included Midnite Rocker, Scorpion, Black Lightning and Diablo VT, as well as manager Don Luigi. In the Jackson area around 1996, J. B. Allen briefly ran a company called Hardcore Championship Wrestling, featuring the likes of Cuban Assassin, Derrick King, Dr. D, Purple Haze and others. In Northeast Mississippi in the late '90s, Leslie Jones's Tupelo-based Intercontinental Wrestling Federation and Keely Rhodes and Rodney Rogers's New Albany–based Southern Championship Wrestling were two heavy hitters. Also, wrestler Rodney "Mega Man" Grimes created his Corinth Wrestling Association (CWA) in 1997. It continues today. A few of the notable stars that CWA brought in included Dusty Rhodes, Road Warrior Animal, Sabu, Kevin Sullivan, Tammy "Sunny" Sytch, The Barbarian, Bobby Eaton and Koko B. Ware.

USWA would be the last true wrestling territory to survive, partially because of the relationship it had developed with the WWF. Most famously, future megastar The Rock spent his first several months in the business, in 1996, wrestling there as Flex Kavana. The next year, however, the territory faced the same fate as its contemporaries. As WCW was at its peak and WWF was on the precipice of reaching heights never before attained by a wrestling organization, the USWA could not compete. Lawler bought Jarrett's half of the company and sold it to an investor named Mark Selker, who had been persuaded to make the deal by a man named Larry Burton. In the fall of 1997, with years of dwindling attendances, the departure of iconic color

Neil "The Real Deal" Taylor hits Barry Wolf with a chair shot at an IWF event. *Tia Howell.*

commentator Dave Brown and under new ownership that lacked wrestling business experience, the final nail was placed in USWA's coffin. WMC TV-5 canceled the company's Saturday morning television program, ending a two-decade run that had begun when Jarrett split from Gulas.

With the demise of USWA, its former booker and devoted Memphis Wrestling fan Randy Hales opened his own promotion, Memphis Power Pro Wrestling (PPW), in early 1998. The company persuaded WMC to begin airing its Saturday morning program, *The Power Hour*. The first show aired on April 18, 1998. The company included a mix of Memphis legends, homegrown talent and rookies under WWF developmental contracts. PPW was the first official developmental territory for the WWF. PPW partnered with Rodney Grimes's CWA for some shows in Corinth and in Tennessee. The promotion visited many of the same places in Mississippi as USWA, with frequent shows at the Lady Luck Casino in Lula and in Clarksdale and Crenshaw, among other towns. USWA alumni who worked for PPW included Jerry Lawler, Bill Dundee, Sid Vicious, Robert Gibson, Koko B. Ware, Brian Christopher, Mabel, Mo, Tracy Smothers, Moondog Spot, Downtown Bruno, Spellbinder, Paul Diamond, King Cobra, Billy Travis, Reggie B. Fine, Rex King, Tony Falk, Brandon Baxter, Ashley Hudson and female wrestlers Jackie Moore and Stacy Carter. Kurt Angle, Baldo (Matt Bloom), Erin O'Grady (Crash Holly), Shawn Stasiak, Steve Bradley and Vic Grimes were some of the WWF developmental wrestlers there. Local talents like Derrick King, Kidd Wikkid, Blade Boudreaux, The Yellow Jacket (Jerry Lawler's youngest son, Kevin), Beau James, Bulldog Raines, Johnny Rotten, Lance Jade, Alan Steel and Ric Havoc rounded out the roster. The company's television show was canceled at the conclusion of its three-year contract. This, along with the company severing its ties with WWF, led to its demise.

A second Memphis-based wrestling company, Memphis Championship Wrestling, also held a WWF developmental deal in the late 1990s and early 2000s. The company, run by wrestler Terry Golden, held events in Corinth, Oxford, Tunica and other cities in the state. Main roster talent like The Acolytes, Raven, Too Cool, Steven Richards, Spike Dudley and Ivory appeared on the company's shows alongside developmental workers like American Dragon (Daniel Bryan), Spanky (Brian Kendrick), Charlie and Russ Haas, The Island Boys, The Mean Street Posse, Joey Matthews (Mercury), K-Krush (R-Truth), Christian York, Seven (Kevin Thorn), The Dupps, Scott Vick, Lance Cade and Victoria. The company ended up closing a few months after Power Pro.

Derrick King in Corinth, Mississippi. He was one of the brightest young stars of PPW and continues to wrestle throughout Mississippi today. *Star Shots by Christy; owner, Christy Harville.*

Perhaps the most unique wrestling company at this time was former rodeo cowboy John Wayne Blough's brainchild, Wrestling for Christ. This "ministry" was created in May 1998 at the First Baptist Church of Richland and toured throughout the state for four years. The faces were biblical heroes or virtues like Peter the Rock, John the Baptist and Still the Phil, while the heels represented vices like Suicide, Drugs (Drugie Dougie), Sexual Impurity and Deception (the Deceiver). The men involved with this organization were not formally trained and said they learned moves by watching videos of the sport.

The two WCW *Uncensored* events were not the worst pay-per-view shows to take place in the state. On October 10, 1999, at Casino Magic in Bay St. Louis, *Heroes of Wrestling* was held, the brainchild of media executive Billy Stone. The veteran-based show was said to have been extremely disorganized. It is most remembered for the drunken antics of Jake "The Snake" Roberts, including miming lewd acts with his snake. From inept announcing to out-of-shape wrestlers, the event was a disaster. Yokozuna, Jim Neidhart, King Kong Bundy, Tully Blanchard, Stan Lane, Jimmy

Jeff Jarrett has appeared in Mississippi through the years with CWA/USWA, WCW, TNA, GFW and a host of independent companies. Here he is appearing for OWO Wrestling on April 30, 2016, in Amory. *Tia Howell.*

Snuka, Bob Orton Jr., One Man Gang, Abdullah the Butcher, Greg Valentine, 2 Cold Scorpio, Marty Jannetty, the Iron Sheik and others wrestled that night. Despite Stone's plan for this to be the first of many such events, *Heroes* was the only wrestling event he ever held.

Between 1998 and 1999, veteran Alabama wrestler Mike Jackson's North American Wrestling Federation ran several shows in Laurel, Sebastapol and other South Mississippi towns. Ken Temple and Tony Wedgeworth were the local promoters in charge of the events. Besides himself, Jackson brought in wrestlers like WCW's Ultimo Dragon and Hector Guerrero, Goldman, California Ken, The Showstopper and former USM baseball player Cliff Wren.

By 2000, WCW was sinking quickly, with plummeting ratings and internal issues. It still managed to draw 8,550 fans for an episode of *Nitro* in Biloxi that April, but Jackson and Tupelo house show attendances fell to between 1,500 and 2,500. During this time, WCW began to push veteran Jeff Jarrett and longtime tag team stars Booker T and Scott Steiner into the main event. A group of wrestlers trained in the company's training center, The Power Plant, also played a significant part in the promotion at this point. Chuck Palumbo, Sean O'Haire and Elix Skipper were a few of these trainees. Biloxi and Tupelo each hosted one final *Nitro* telecast in February 2001, just one month before WCW's sale to the WWF.

7

WWE RULES THE RING, THE RISE OF "OUTLAW" WRESTLING AND THE OUTLOOK FOR THE FUTURE

With WCW out of the picture, the newly renamed World Wrestling Entertainment (WWE) became the unquestioned leader throughout the Magnolia State and the world. Within the first fifteen months after purchasing WCW, WWE visited Biloxi, Hattiesburg and Jackson for non-televised shows and drew 7,450 fans for a live *Smackdown* telecast in Tupelo. Big names on the card included Triple H, Chris Jericho and Kurt Angle. Jerry Lawler, who had been working for WWE for almost a decade, defeated Albert in the opening match of the card. Between 2003 and 2007, the company visited Mississippi a whopping thirteen times, going to Biloxi (four), Hattiesburg (three), Jackson (three) and Tupelo (three). John Cena, Shawn Michaels, Randy Orton, CM Punk, an aging Ric Flair, Batista, Chris Benoit, Kane, Rob Van Dam, Eddie Guerrero, Big Show, Booker T, John Bradshaw Layfield, Bobby Lashley, Edge, Sabu, Umaga, the Great Khali, Matt and Jeff Hardy and "divas" like Trish Stratus, Lita and Molly Holly appeared with WWE in the state in that span. Business was down in those years, and crowds measured between 1,500 and 3,000 for non-televised events.

As an alternative to WWE, Jerry and Jeff Jarrett created NWA Total Nonstop Action (TNA) in 2002. It featured ex-WCW stars, departed WWE wrestlers and a host of up-and-coming talents. TNA first came to Mississippi in 2007. Between then and its last trip to the state in 2014, the company visited Mississippi at least twenty times. Besides holding events in Biloxi,

Pure Destruction (Brody and Cody Hawk) take DC Daniel Cross up for a back body drop.
Star Shots by Christy; owner, Christy Harville.

Hattiesburg, Jackson and Tupelo, TNA also came to towns like Corinth, Greenwood, Southaven and Vicksburg. The promotion even held its 2008 *Slammiversary* pay-per-view in Southaven, drawing approximately six thousand people. It also filmed an episode of the company's *Impact Wrestling* television show in Tupelo. Besides these larger events, crowds for TNA shows in the state ranged from three hundred to two thousand people, still showing that the sport was in decline. Stars who worked for TNA in Mississippi included Sting, Kevin Nash, Scott Steiner, Kurt Angle, Rob Van Dam, Booker T, Jeff Jarrett, A.J. Styles, Abyss, Rhino, Samoa Joe, Christian Cage, Kip James (Billy Gunn), Matt and Jeff Hardy, James Storm, Robert Roode, Christopher Daniels, Consequences Creed (Xavier Woods), Tommy Dreamer, Bully Ray (Bubba Ray Dudley), Brother Devon (D-Von Dudley), Mr. Anderson, Bobby Lashley, Ethan Carter III, Magnus (Nick Aldis), Chavo Guerrero Jr., D-Lo Brown, Austin Aries and "Knockouts" like Awesome Kong, Daffney, Velvet Sky, Mickie James, Gail Kim and Tara. The company changed its name to Impact Wrestling and continues operating, though Mississippi does not seem to be a part of the company's immediate plans. Impact wrestlers like Ace Austin, Su Yung and Johnny Swinger occasionally appear on independent shows around the state.

Right: Jessie Belle getting the better of former TNA Knockout and Ring of Honor performer Taeler Hendrix at the Isle of Capri Casino Hotel on May 7, 2016. *Tia Howell*.

Opposite: Former WWE superstar Sasha Banks, who now wrestles for New Japan as Mercedes Moné. *Wikimedia Commons*.

Between 2008 and 2017, WWE appeared twenty-two times in the state, including six televised events. During this time, business for the company picked up a bit, with crowds averaging from 2,500 to 7,000 in the state. Stars who had made the company prosperous in the Attitude era and before would gradually begin to shorten their schedules or retire, with names like John Cena, Randy Orton, CM Punk, Big Show, Edge, Rey Mysterio and The Miz leading the way into the 2010s, after which stars like Roman Reigns, Seth Rollins, Dean Ambrose, Sheamus, Daniel Bryan, Bray Wyatt, Cody Rhodes, Braun Strowman, Finn Bálor, Alberto Del Rio, Rusev, The New Day and longtime TNA main eventer AJ Styles assumed major roles with the company. An emphasis also began to be placed on women's wrestling at this time, and wrestlers like Becky Lynch, Charlotte, Naomi, Sasha Banks, Beth Phoenix, AJ Lee, Paige, The Bella Twins, Nia Jax, Alexa Bliss, Natalya, Tamina Snuka and Alicia Fox would have matches in the state. In 2017, WWE's developmental brand, NXT, also made a couple of trips in the state, both in Southaven. These shows featured future main roster talent like Bobby Roode, Aleister Black, Johnny Gargano, Tommaso Ciampa, Andrade, Ricochet, The Street Profits, Adam Cole, Asuka, Ruby Riott, Lacey Evans and Sonya Deville.

In the middle and late years of the first decade of the twenty-first century, an abundance of small promotions popped up in the state. It seemed that almost every wrestler wanted to try his luck at promoting events. Notable

North Mississippi companies at the time included the following: veteran Wayne Blaylock's Mississippi Ultimate Wrestling Alliance and The Future of Wrestling, which operated from the middle of the first decade of the twenty-first century until 2012; Billy Russ and Tony Watts's Xtreme Outlaw Wrestling, which enjoyed a long run in the northern part of the state; Dwayne Huckaba's Deep South Championship Wrestling; Golden Triangle Wrestling around the West Point area; Charlie Parks's IWA Championship Wrestling in Southaven; Maximum Championship Wrestling; and Jerry

Lawler's Memphis Wrestling. The small town of Booneville has a solid argument for being the current wrestling capital of that portion of the state. Marty Cooksey and Edith Poole ran Mississippi Championship Wrestling in the town from 2000 to 2002. A few years later, promoter Sammy McGee ran a company called JWS in the same building. Edith Poole took over the promotion in June 2008 and changed its name to Extreme Professional Wrestling (EPW). This is the state's longest-running weekly wrestling show in the state. Veteran North Mississippi wrestler Neil "The Real Deal" Taylor is currently in charge of the promotion.

Some of the stars of North Mississippi wrestling in the 2000s included Taylor, "Boogie Woogie Boy" Gary Valiant, Syn (Jacksyn Crowley), Suicide (Otis Crowley), Big Daddy Storm, "War Machine" Gene Jackson, Nick Grimes, "Bad Attitude" Tony Dabbs, "Extreme" Brett Michaels, Mike Jones/Scott Porteau, The Asylum, Bonecrusher, Kross Mann, Sarge O'Riley, Motley Cruz, Dustin "Five" Starr, Samoan Raja, Dangerous David Cox, Chris Chaos, Dirty Sanchez, Devon Raynes, Precious, Chop, Chazz Stone, Fusion, Casanova Kid, Curly Moe, The Pink Flamingos, Mark Mayhem, Justin Rhodes, Max Steele, Vinnie the Blade, Josh Matthews, Jay Webb, Chris Styles, Tysin Starr, Keylo Green, Dirty Terrell Moore, Shawn Reed, Hallow, LSD, Psykotikk, The Baron Malkevian, DC Daniel Cross, Steven Harmon, "Albino Rhino" Dustin Burcham, Maxx Corbin, A.N.T., Eldrick Hines, Cody Melton, JR Mauler, Bubba Boudreaux, Hoss Williams, Kaleb Kastle, David Andrews, Soultaker, Blazing Star, Jose Guerrero, Justin Reed, Robert Rose, Jake Prentiss, Galon Ray, Andy2Dandy, Pokerface, Chris Rocker, Cameron Valentine, Dalton Storm, D.J. Stunner, Chris Stevens, Buzz Harley, Cymba, Armageddon, Kayden and Xander Cross, Chris Fontaine, Malik "The Great," BJ Fuller, Slammer, Damion Rage, Danny Morris, Chris Austin, Chris Kilgore, Tatt2, Chris Lexxus, Big Daddy Neno, Candyman, Ghost Rider, Drew Donovan, Black Pearl, Bishop and Dell Tucker, Funky Freddy Feelgood and Erick Hayes. In addition were ladies Su Yung, Tasha Simone, Josie, Misty James, Brandi Wine, Diane Von Hoffman, Sin D, BB, Queen Destiny and Lil' Bit. Legends like Jerry Lawler, Bill Dundee, Grandmaster Sexay, Big Daddy V, Rikishi, Jimmy Hart, Doug Gilbert, Downtown Bruno and the Rock 'n' Roll Express continued to make appearances at that time, and many of those are still appearing sporadically at the time of this publication.

Louisiana-based Bayou Independent Wrestling has been a steady presence in the state since it first appeared here in 2009. The company is run by real estate agent Josh Newell, who works tirelessly to promote his brand. Other

Above: Kross Mann throws a fireball at Bonecrusher. These two men have been instrumental in helping *EPW* become the state's longest-running weekly wrestling show. *Star Shots by Christy; owner, Christy Harville.*

Left: Jerry Lawler (*right*) and Jimmy Hart (*left*) have been a major part of North Mississippi wrestling for the past fifty years. Both men continue to make sporadic appearances at wrestling events in the state. *Star Shots by Christy; owner, Christy Harville.*

important promotions in the central and southern portions of the state late in the first decade of the new century included Xtreme Impact Wrestling in Pascagoula, Southland Wrestling and Pro Wrestling Valor in Poplarville and the Mississippi Combat Alliance in Natchez. The Alabama Wrestling Federation also ran shows around Lucedale. Some of the most prolific wrestlers in the area included Steve Anthony, "The Monster" Clarice, Wade Garrett, Kent Truth, Apocalypse, Adrian Whisper, Vordell Walker, The Mountain Man, Nathan Crown, Xion, The Goliath Kid, Jason Dukes, Andy Dalton, Trainwreck, Dylan Hale, John Saxon, The Reaper, The Scorpion, The Alabama Jawjacker, The Convict, Eric Wayne, Kirk King, Micah Taylor, Cool J Steel, Hi-Jinx, Jason Vayne, Indestructible LC, Nathan Buzzby, Carlos D'Angelo, Randy Riggins, Rikki Roberts, Mr. Jimmy King, General Payne, 2 Quick, J.D. Scoundrel, Bonez, Yellow Hornet, Johnny Reed, Johnny Stevens, Joe Milo, Crazy Cody Krueger, B.J. Sullivan, Sassy Vegas and ladies the Irresistible Danielle and the Lovely Layla.

In the 2010s, several companies operated in the northern portion of the state, including the following: Tony Dabbs's Tupelo-based Allied Independent Wrestling Federation (AIWF) Intense; Dirty Terrell Moore's Outlaw Wrestling Organization; Dustin Starr's Memphis Wrestling; Action Packed Wrestling in Columbus; Southaven's South's Greatest Wrestling Association; and Independent Championship Wrestling, former territory star Ray Rowland's daughter Tonya's company with Tina Gant. Wrestlers like Marko Stunt, Walker Hayes, Danny Dollar, "Big Swole," Justin Cole, Steven Styles, Judas Thorn, Stagger Lee, "The Showcase" Chris Adams, Dirty Dustin Dundee, Devon Day, Ju Ju Bokor, P.K. Ripper, Knockout Kid, Jerry Adams, Nathan Lawler, Shannon Lee, T.J. Riley, David Eckos, Joker, Big Ace, The Moose, Jett Hero, Mike Realz, Bishop Cage, V-Man, Matt Storm, Vin Vader, Bull Bronson, American G.I., Jason Vaughn, Super Brown, ATK, Will Sharp, Cody Only, Idolbane, Memphis Monroe, Nathan Aulridge and ladies Venus Starr, Auburn Thunder, Nikki Lane, Jessica London, Paris Kelly, Rebecca Raze, Dirty Diana Taylor and Cassandra Golden were among the local stars of that decade.

The most notable upstarts in South and Central Mississippi in the 2010s were Pro Wrestling Ego, based around Brandon; Diamond Championship Wrestling on the coast; Kiln's Powerslam Productions; and AIWF Mid South in Clinton. Notable competitors who worked in that half of the state included the following: Angel Camacho, Krypt Keeper, Rob Love, Wess Warren, Bam Bam Malone, Barrett Brown, The Bowser Boys, Aaron Hart, Danny Chance, The Charlie West, Draven Lee, Rob Allen, Dynamite

Left: Bayou Independent Wrestling is one of the top promotions in Central Mississippi. One of the top stables there is Southern Royalty. Pictured are, from *left to right*, members Nightmare Jeremiah, Rob Love and Angel Camacho. *Kristen Newell*.

Below: *Back row, left to right*: "Xtreme" Brett Michaels (The Gun Show), "Studd" Mike Jones (Scott Porteau) and "Bad Attitude" Tony Dabbs. *Front row (kneeling)*: "Dirty" Terrell Moore. *Tia Howell*.

Jay Andrews, Sergeant Carlos Socorro, Nightmare Jeremiah, Jaykus Plisken, JD Jenkins, Curt Matthews, Joey Abel, Lukas Frost, Frankie Thomas, Mike Dell, Ling Phan, Chance Auren, Calvin Rose, Reggie Matthews, O'Shay Edwards, Blake Wilder, Jake Jameson, Wes Adams, Joe Kane, Rumble O'Reilly, Matt Lancie, Kobra King, Steve O'Malley, Rey Fury, Obadiah, Korey Konstantine and ladies Thunder Kitty, Myka Madrid, Kandi Jewel, Sarah Summers, Rockelle Vaughn, Emmy Camacho and Bristol Hayle.

WWE would continue making sporadic trips into Biloxi, Jackson and Tupelo, though it has been since 2016 that the company has filmed any television in the state. Tupelo was scheduled to host a WWE event in 2020, but the COVID outbreak led to the event's cancellation. Jackson is the only city in the state the company has visited since that time, with three visits. As of this writing, it has been over four years since WWE came to Biloxi and three and a half years since the company came to Tupelo. Rumors of Vince McMahon's impending sale of

Ted DiBiase Jr. left WWE in 2013. He made a few appearances for Mississippi independent promotion Pro Wrestling EGO in 2016 and 2017. *Wikimedia Commons.*

the company, potentially to international entities, have made the company's future cloudy. If the sale were to happen, the entire landscape of professional wrestling could be affected, whether positive or negative remains to be seen.

On January 1, 2019, wrestling fan and businessman Tony Khan created All Elite Wrestling (AEW), which automatically became the number-two wrestling company in the United States due to its resources. The company somehow took wrestling more and less seriously than the WWE. The moves done by many of the wrestlers on AEW's roster are often remarkable and eclipse those done in the WWE, but many of the characters are often more unrealistic than anything offered by WWE. Led by former WWE and WCW star Chris Jericho, the company originally featured "indy darlings" like The Young Bucks, Kenny Omega, Joey Janela, MJF and

The Crowleys—Otis (*far left*) and Jacksyn (*far right*)—and Walker Hayes (*center*) make their way to the ring for a match for VIP Championship Wrestling in Tupelo, Mississippi, on July 24, 2021. *Star Shots by Christy; owner, Christy Harville.*

Adam "Hangman" Page, alongside former WWE talents like Cody and Dusti Rhodes, PAC, Jake Hager and, later, Jon Moxley. The company appeared at the Landers Center in Southaven on January 8, 2020, hosting a celebration of Memphis wrestling legends. The show drew 3,100 fans, which was on the low end of normal for the promotion at the time. The company has not appeared in the state since, though its limited schedule

Left: "Real American" Trace Lee Hunt comes at Jason Genesis with a flying shoulder tackle. *Star Shots by Christy; owner, Christy Harville.*

Right: "Dirty" Diana Taylor is one of the top female wrestlers in Mississippi. *Star Shots by Christy; owner, Christy Harville.*

could explain why. It seems that the only way Mississippians can expect to see much AEW live is to venture out of the state.

Currently, there is a large array of promotions around the state, such as long-running EPW, Bayou Independent Wrestling (BIW), Outlaw Wrestling Organization (OWO) and Memphis Wrestling, along with "Hollywood" Jimmy Blaylock's successful VIP Championship Wrestling, Louisiana-based Pro Wrestling 225, Gil Culkin and Steve Starr's new Legacy Championship Wrestling, the upstart Crossroads Wrestling and Memphis' Total Wrestling Xplosion. Area veterans like The Gun Show, The Crowleys, Barry Wolf and others join younger stars like Vladimir Koloff, Trace Lee Hunt, Jason Genesis, Brandon Young, Marko Harris, Gio Savage, Van Vicious, Colton Cage, K Toomer, The Hot Shots, K-Swiss, Logan Stunt, Perky Will, Bryce Dancy, RJW and Zay Washington to create a healthy environment for Mississippi independent wrestling. Rookies like Ingomar's Big John Dalton, Tupelo's Ray Collins and others are hoping that the future will belong to them. Many of these wrestlers recently joined the acting world on the third season of NBC's *Young Rock*.

With the WWF's future in doubt and AEW showing no signs of making Mississippi a priority, Mississippians must continue to rely on independent wrestling, unless they want to make the trek to one of the large cities in Alabama, Louisiana or Tennessee, where bigger shows are often held. Thankfully, the independent scene in the state continues to thrive. It remains to be seen whether or not the sport will ever again reach the popularity it saw in the late '90s and early 2000s. Though wrestling may have given up its spot as one of the most popular sports in the state, now falling somewhere behind football, baseball and basketball, it remains a fun distraction from the mundane and a favorite among a diverse group of people made up of feisty grandmothers, energetic preteens and every age group in between. In the melting pot that is the wrestling arena, in whatever town you choose, you will find a cross-section of America. Inside that building, divisive factors like race, sexual orientation and socioeconomic status are put aside, and all groups sit, stand and chant side by side, cheering on the forces of good in their continued battles with ever-present evil.

PART IV

FAMOUS MISSISSIPPI WRESTLERS AND WRESTLING PERSONALITIES

THE CURTIS/CULKIN FAMILY

Jack, Jack Jr. and Randy Curtis, George and Gil Culkin

Because of their long and storied history with the sport in the state, it is appropriate to refer to the Curtis/Culkin family as the first family of Mississippi wrestling. Elbert James "Jack" Curtis was born on April 17, 1911, in Vicksburg. He began wrestling in the South Texas area near the Mexican border in 1931 and wrestled for almost thirty years. A smaller wrestler, Curtis was described by the *Clarion-Ledger* as "fast" and "smart." He spent his entire career as a babyface, or fan favorite, even earning the nickname "Gentleman" because of his adherence to the rules. He was also nicknamed "The San Antonio Flash" early in his career because of his speed. One of Curtis's signature moves was the bulldogging headlock, known today as simply a bulldog. He also liked using the airplane spin and the chin flip, which he is credited with inventing.

Though he started his career in Texas, the territory Curtis most frequented was Billy Romanoff's, in Jack's home state of Mississippi. He wrestled in nearly every state in the continental United States and in Ontario, Canada, and engaged in a handful of trips into Mexico. In fact, he wrestled in front of six thousand people in one of the first wrestling events in Mexico City, facing Yaqui Joe. Besides Joe, some of Curtis's most frequent opponents in the early portion of his career were Silent Rattan, Sheik Mar Allah and Joe Reno. He gained the most publicity from his time spent wrestling in the Chicago area in the late 1930s, with his name frequently appearing in newspapers around the country.

The Curtis Brothers (Jack and George [Culkin]). *Gil Culkin.*

In 1938, Jack began his rivalry with Rex Mobley. The two wrestled throughout the Southeast, trading many different titles back and forth. They even occasionally teamed together. Jack was World Light Heavyweight Champion nine times. He also held numerous regional Light Heavyweight and Junior Heavyweight Championships. By the 1950s, he had added some bulk and won the Southern and Louisiana Heavyweight Titles. In 1939, Curtis briefly served as the promoter for wrestling events in Yazoo City before deciding to concentrate on wrestling. He accumulated many wins in his career, including a streak of several months while wrestling for Nick Gulas and Roy Welch, in which he grabbed wins over Red Roberts, Yaqui Joe, Herb Welch, Oki Shikina, George Sauer and others.

A second member of this famous family entered the wrestling business in 1944. Elva George Culkin, Jack's younger half brother, was born on April 12, 1926, also in Vicksburg. He started wrestling at the local YMCA and had his first professional match with veteran wrestler Joe Kopecky, who defeated Culkin in only four minutes. For a large portion of his career, he wrestled as "George Curtis" and was acknowledged as Jack's brother. George began wrestling throughout Mississippi for Billy Romanoff and around the southeastern United States. Quite early on, George found himself competing with fellow Vicksburg-area wrestler Henry Harrell. Jack and George often teamed up as the Curtis Brothers. They were one of the very first brother teams in wrestling and had success, especially in their later careers.

In 1946, George Curtis set out on his own. Like his brother, he spent much of his time wrestling in Texas and other midwestern states. He also spent time wrestling in the Pacific Northwest and Vancouver, Canada. On October 31, 1949, the Curtis Brothers teamed up to win a tag team tournament in Tulsa, defeating Speedy and Johnny LaRance, as well as Al Galento and Angelo Savoldi. In the early 1950s, George feuded with Ali Pasha and Bobby Segura and teamed up with former World Heavyweight Boxing Champion Primo Carnera on a handful of occasions. Like Jack, George moved from smaller weight divisions to heavyweight in the 1950s, holding several singles titles, such as Mississippi Heavyweight Champion.

Jack and George would begin teaming up regularly in 1951, when they won their first of several different Southern Tag Team Titles. After a run together in Mississippi and Louisiana, they had stints in Mid-Atlantic, Georgia and Florida. In Texas, they won their first of two Southwestern States Tag Team Titles on October 1, 1953, by defeating Ivan Kalmikoff and Ace Abbott in a tournament final.

Also in 1953, yet another member of the family, Jack Curtis Jr.—sometimes referred to as Jackie in his early career—made his in-ring debut. Jack Jr. was born on April 16, 1935, also in Vicksburg. He served in the U.S. Air Force during the Korean War and was stationed in Wichita Falls, Texas, for a good portion of his time. Among his first matches were six-man tag team contests in which the three Curtises defeated the combinations of Wild Bill Steddum, Mr. X #1 and Mr. X #2, and Sailor Moran, Jack Lozano and George (Lefty) Thomas around Christmastime. He did this for a few years in a row, perhaps on some type of holiday leave from the military. Around this time, at forty-five years of age, Jack Sr. began taking fewer bookings. Also around this period of the mid-to-late 1950s, it appears that Jack Sr. and George headed a group that promoted wrestling in the state.

In March 1957, Jack Jr. began wrestling full-time, spending most of the year in the Mississippi area. At this point, George and Jack Jr. began to team up frequently, even holding the Southeastern Tag Team Titles for almost four months that year. Later in 1957, the two Jacks won the same titles for their first of two times. This would be each of the team's only titles together. After Jack and Jack Jr. won their second tag titles in 1959, Jack, at the age of forty-eight, fully retired from the ring. A year later, George also retired, going to work as a deputy sheriff in Warren County. In the late 1960s, he would lose a race for sheriff of the same county.

In 1960, Jack Jr. began to come into his own. He spent time working for Leroy McGuirk's territory, where he held the Arkansas Junior Heavyweight Title for a month, before moving to Durham and enrolling at the University of North Carolina. While there, he wrestled for the Mid-Atlantic territory. When he started wrestling for Mid-Atlantic, Jack won the Southern Tag Team Titles there with Ray Villmer, titles they would lose to the Vachons two months later.

Thomas Randolph "Randy" Curtis was born in Vicksburg in 1939. He was the son of Jack and Doris Curtis and the younger brother of Jack Curtis Jr. After graduating high school in 1957, Randy joined the U.S. Air Force. Before his retirement from the military in 1987, he had been a part of the air force, army and national guard. Randy began training with his father in 1959 and debuted in the ring by March 1961, wrestling throughout the state alongside the likes of Earl Guess and Wild Bill Steddum. In 1962, Randy and Jack Jr. teamed up in the Fields brothers' Gulf Coast territory and on other smaller shows in Mississippi. After this, Jack Jr. found a home wrestling for the Tri-State (McGuirk) territory, and in 1963, he graduated from Mississippi

College. Randy spent some time wrestling in Georgia, but he did not wrestle nearly as frequently as his other family members. In 1968, George sold a majority of his land to join up with McGuirk to bring big wrestling shows to Mississippi. In the beginning of his new venture, George came out of in-ring retirement. He participated in a battle royal, teamed with Gorgeous George Jr. against Jim Osbourne and Jerry Miller and teamed with Jerry Brisco. He wrestled a light schedule through early 1970, when he hung up his trunks for good.

In 1969, Randy Curtis began his most successful period of wrestling, spending much of the next two years racking up wins in Mid-Atlantic over the likes of Ronnie and Terry Garvin, Pedro Valdez and Billy Hines. Jack Jr. wrestled around the Southeast and Midwest during these years, winning the Tri-State version of the Mississippi Heavyweight Title, which he held for several months. In November 1970, Randy began a monthlong tour overseas with the Japan Wrestling Association. There, he faced Antonio Inoki, Hiro Matsuda, the Great Kojika and others.

When Randy got back to the United States, he wrestled for the Tri-State territory, where he was crowned the Louisiana Heavyweight Champion. He also spent more time in Mid-Atlantic before working in Ann Gunkel's All-South Wrestling Alliance in Georgia and Nick Gulas and Roy Welch's NWA Mid-America, where he held the Southern Tag Team Titles twice with Lorenzo Parente. Randy retired from the ring in 1973. Besides his military service, he also worked in several retail positions before opening his own antiques store, Indian relic museum and military surplus store. Tommy and his family made their home in Rockingham, North Carolina.

In 1974, a final family member, Gil Culkin, George's son, entered the business. George Gilman Curtis was born on February 19, 1954, in Vicksburg. Unlike his family members, Gil worked only on the business end of things and not in the ring. After attending Hinds Community College, he began work on the railroad before his father asked him to consider helping in the business. In 1977, Jack Jr. finished his in-ring career working McGuirk shows. Around this time, George and Gil chose to cut ties with "Cowboy" Bill Watts and Leroy McGuirk. Jack Jr. stayed with Watts and McGuirk because his job with them provided him with financial stability. Besides wrestling, George worked in the chancery's clerk's office for J.L. "Peewee" Hudgins before being elected circuit clerk of Warren County in 1973. He served in this position until 1988, when he retired.

The territory war between the Culkins and Bill Watts lasted from October 1977 until August 1979. The Culkins' promotion, called International

Championship Wrestling, is the only successful Mississippi-only territory in history. Afterward, they and Bill Watts reconciled, and the Culkins and Watts continued booking Tri-State, Mid-South and UWF cards in the state through 1987, when Watts sold his company to Jim Crockett Promotions. George and Gil occasionally booked World Class Championship Wrestling and Continental Championship Wrestling in the state through 1989, when they left the business. Jack Jr. continued to pop up in promotions in the late 1980s and 1990s, such as CCW, Five Star Wrestling, Deep South Wrestling and Southern Championship Wrestling.

During his career outside the ring, Jack ran several different types of stores, including a fireworks stand, a military surplus store and a discount grocery store. He also spent twenty-five years on the board of directors for the River City Rescue Mission. Gil worked as a criminal investigator for the Warren County District Attorney and owned several small businesses himself. Jack Curtis Sr. died in an automobile accident in 1989. On February 26, 2005, George Culkin passed away, and sixteen years later, on January 2, 2021, Jack Curtis Jr. died. In 2022, Gil decided that the time had come for him to give the business another try. Along with Mississippi independent wrestling veteran Steve Starr, he opened Legacy Championship Wrestling, a small company that works with schools and clubs to help them raise money. As the name of Gil's new promotion implies, the contributions this family has made to Mississippi wrestling since the 1930s have been tremendous and unlike any other.

9

THE DIBIASE FAMILY

Ted, Mike, Ted Jr. and Brett

Ted DiBiase was born on January 8, 1954, in Miami Beach, Florida. His mother was a professional wrestler, going by the name Helen Hild. After she and Ted's birth father divorced, she met wrestler "Iron" Mike DiBiase, and the two were wed. This is who Ted calls "Dad." In 1969, Mike died of a heart attack in the ring in Lubbock, Texas. Ted attended college and played football at West Texas State University in Canyon, Texas, but left before his senior year when mounting injuries put his football career in jeopardy. While in college, he began training in the ring with the Funk family and worked first as a referee.

On December 21, 1973, after his sophomore season, he married Jaynet, a childhood friend with whom he had become reacquainted in college. In June 1974, Ted wrestled his first match, teaming with Terry Funk and Dick Murdoch to defeat J.J. Dillon and The Patriots. He spent the following summer touring with Bill Watts's Mid-South territory, a promotion with which he spent a large part of his early career, having four separate runs there and winning several North American Heavyweight and Tag Team Titles. He worked mostly babyface in his first several years in the business. He also spent time in the Funks' Amarillo territory and Bob Geigel's St. Louis territory in his first few years, as well as making trips overseas for Giant Baba's All-Japan Wrestling. In nearly every promotion, Ted held one or more championships.

Around that time, Ted and Jaynet became pregnant with a child they named Mike, after Ted's dad. While working in Amarillo, Ted made an

"Million Dollar Man" Ted DiBiase. *Wikimedia Commons.*

appearance in the movie *Paradise Alley* starring Sylvester Stallone. In early 1978, Ted began working for Sam Muchnick's prestigious St. Louis territory. There, he feuded with Harley Race, the reigning NWA World Heavyweight Champion. The next year, he went to work for Vince McMahon Sr.'s World Wide Wrestling Federation. Ted was brought in as the North American Heavyweight Champion, which was renamed the Intercontinental Title after it was won by Pat Patterson. In the WWWF, Ted teamed with Andre the Giant, Ivan Putski and Tito Santana. He even faced Hulk Hogan in Hogan's first match for the company.

Around this time, Ted and Jaynet divorced, after which young Mike would spend most of his time with his mother. Besides Mid-South, Ted spent much of the early 1980s in Atlanta's Georgia Championship Wrestling, where he again won multiple titles and notably feuded with Tommy Rich. While there, Ted met and married his second wife, Melanie. The two were wed on December 31, 1981. On January 1, 1980, Ted turned heel for the first time in his career after using a foreign object to defeat his friend Junkyard Dog. On November 8, 1982, while still working for Watts, Ted's second son, Ted Jr., was born.

In the mid-1980s Ted relocated his family to Clinton, Mississippi, near his wife's parents. This happened during his last run with Mid-South, in which Ted feuded extensively with Hacksaw Jim Duggan and formed a successful team with "Dr. Death" Steve Williams. After Ted left Mid-South for the final time, Jim Crockett Promotions and Vince McMahon Jr.'s World Wrestling Federation got wrapped up in a bit of a bidding war for Ted's services. He decided on Vince's offer to become the Million Dollar Man, a character that would change Ted's life forever. This event coincided with the birth of his third son, Brett. Brett was the only Mississippi-born DiBiase child, entering the world on March 16, 1988.

As the Million Dollar Man, Ted was paired with former Memphis wrestler Soul Train Jones, who was brought in as DiBiase's bodyguard, Virgil. Ted's biggest triumph came at *WrestleMania IV*, where a fourteen-man tournament was held to name a new WWF World Heavyweight Champion. Andre the

Giant had recently defeated champion Hulk Hogan in a match and sold the title to DiBiase, in a move that vacated the title and led to the tournament. Ted made the finals of the tournament, defeating "Hacksaw" Jim Duggan and Don Muraco before losing to "Macho Man" Randy Savage in the finals. He would spend the majority of the rest of that year teaming with Andre against Hogan and Savage. He was also crowned King of the Ring that year.

After being unsuccessful in his attempts to secure the WWF World Championship, the Million Dollar Man created his own belt, the diamond-adorned "Million Dollar Title," in 1989. DiBiase feuded with Jake Roberts and Dusty Rhodes before having a series of matches with former bodyguard Virgil, who had grown tired of DiBiase's constant berating. In late 1991, Ted was teamed with Irwin R. Schyster in a duo called Money Inc. Between 1992 and 1993, the team won three WWF World Tag Team Titles and feuded with teams like The Legion of Doom, The Steiner Brothers and The Natural Disasters. While working as the Million Dollar Man, Ted partied hard and was often unfaithful to his wife. In spring 1992, she learned of his misdeeds and was on the verge of ending their twelve-year marriage. However, with time and Ted working to change his ways, Melanie was able to forgive him. Ted wrestled his last match for the WWF at *SummerSlam 1993*, as he did not wish to be tempted by his previous vices on the road. Later that year, a neck injury ended his in-ring career for good.

In early 1994, Ted began working as a commentator and manager for WWF, eventually concentrating solely on his managerial duties. As the leader of the Million Dollar Corporation between 1994 and 1996, Ted managed Sid Vicious, Bam Bam Bigelow, King Kong Bundy, Tatanka, Kama, Nikolai Volkoff and others. The stable's most notable feuds were their matches with The Undertaker, Bigelow's *WrestleMania* match with NFL legend Lawrence Taylor and Sid Vicious's main event run against then-champion Diesel. DiBiase also managed Steve Austin when he arrived in the WWF in December 1995. In May 1996, Ted left the company altogether, again wishing to concentrate on his family life.

On August 26, 1996, Ted debuted for World Championship Wrestling as the fourth member of the New World Order. He was brought in to be its manager but became just another member of the crowded group when Eric Bischoff inserted himself in that role. In August 1997, Ted turned face and managed Ray Traylor and the Steiner Brothers, whom he led to two runs with the WCW World Tag Team Titles. In 1999, he left WCW and began concentrating on his ministry, sharing his testimony around the country. Ted was ordained as a Baptist minister on February 27, 2000. He called his organization The Heart of David Ministries. His son Ted Jr. was an excellent high school football player, and Brett excelled at soccer.

From April 2005 through October 2006, Ted went back to the company now known as WWE, working as an advisor to the creative team and a producer. Though he continued to make occasional appearances for the WWE and smaller wrestling companies after that, he spent most of his time working on his ministry.

All three of Ted's sons would spend time in the wrestling business. Mike and Ted Jr. entered the business around the same time, and both had their first match on July 8, 2006. They were initially trained by Chris Youngblood before going to Harley Race's wrestling school. The two mainly wrestled for Race's World League Wrestling their first several months, often teaming as the DiBiase Brothers. Mike won the tag team titles there with Wade Chism. In early 2007, Ted Jr. and Mike were offered a spot on tour with Japan's Pro Wrestling NOAH promotion, though only Ted Jr. could make the trip, as Mike had sustained a serious knee injury just prior. When Ted Jr. got back, he was offered a WWE developmental deal. He worked with developmental territory Florida Championship Wrestling (FCW), where he won the Southern Heavyweight Championship. He debuted in the WWE in January 2008 and won two tag team titles that year. He wrestled for the company until 2013, leaving to spend more time with his family. He went into the business field when he left the ring.

Mike returned from his injury late in 2007. He won the Professional Wrestling Federation Tag Team Titles and began working for NWA promotions in the Midwest, winning the NWA North American Heavyweight title that year. In 2008, he also won the NWA Texas Heavyweight Title, before being stripped of it that same year. He held the North American Title almost seventeen months before losing it in April 2009 and retiring from the ring soon after. Youngest brother Brett started his career with FCW on a developmental deal with WWE. There, he formed a tag team with Joe Hennig called The Fortunate Sons and won the FCW Tag Team Titles. Because of lingering knee issues, he left wrestling in 2011. Ted Jr. and Brett wrestled a couple of matches for Mississippi-based independent promotion Pro Wrestling Ego in 2016 and 2017. In February 2023, Brett returned to the ring with Battlezone Championship Wrestling. In 2017, Ted and Ted Jr. worked together to release a documentary, *The Price of Fame*, which details the spiritual journeys of both wrestlers.

Ted, Ted Jr., Brett and some of their respective companies were named as defendants in a lawsuit that has been termed "Mississippi's largest public corruption case." The suit alleges that the Mississippi Department of Human Services misappropriated millions of federal dollars provided to fund the state's Temporary Assistance for Needy Families program by granting companies and nonprofits funds for ineligible services, many of which were never completed at all. Notably, Brett DiBiase pled guilty in 2020 to a felony fraud charge for receiving $48,000 through deceptive means and again to a federal conspiracy charge in March 2023. Brett has admitted to fraudulently submitting documentation and being paid for work that was never done because of his stint in a rehab center in Malibu for opioid addiction. Brett could serve up to five years in prison for the federal charge. Court dates for the other DiBiases have not happened at the time of this publication, though the men remain actively tied to the scandal.

10

DOWNTOWN BRUNO /
HARVEY WIPPLEMAN

Bruno Laurer was born in Pennsylvania on October 27, 1965, but he is by all accounts (including his own) a Mississippian. His mother had family there, and he found himself enjoying his time in the state and vowing to live there one day. In 1979, thirteen-year-old Laurer met wrestler Lord Jonathan Boyd, who helped him break into the business. Bruno's first managerial job was working for Kentucky promoter Dale Mann's Mid-Continental Wrestling after lying about his experience. Once he came back from the tour, he approached Geeto Mongol, who ran a wrestling school and promotion near Laurer's family home. Exaggerating his experience again, Bruno began helping Geeto promote shows and managing as "Dr. Lennard Spazzinsky." Afterward, Laurer worked independent shows across Pennsylvania, the Midwest and Appalachia before landing at Hawaii's Polynesian Pacific Championship Wrestling (PPCW), where he dubbed himself "Downtown Bruno." In Hawaii, he worked in the office, managed some lower-tier wrestlers and put up the ring for events. When business slowed down for PPCW and his paychecks began to shrink, Bruno left the territory and returned to Pennsylvania.

After seeing Jimmy Hart on WWF programming, Laurer began persistently calling Jerry Lawler and Randy Hales to try to obtain a job with Memphis' CWA Wrestling. He began there in October 1986, with most not expecting him to last long with the company. Bruno impressed Lawler and soon became the prominent heel manager there, managing Tony Falk, The Rock 'n' Roll RPMs, the Moondogs, Big Bubba, Tojo Yamamoto, Pat

Tanaka, the Kelly Twins, Paul Diamond, Man Mountain Link and others.

In 1987, Bruno's top spot was given to a brash New York manager named Paul E. Dangerously. Bruno was relegated to the lower card and left the company. After CWA, Bruno briefly worked for Bob Geigel in Kansas City managing The Batten Twins. He then contacted Continental Championship Wrestling, based in Dothan, Alabama, and was offered a position by booker Robert Fuller as the manager of the Mad Max–inspired character Lord Humongous, whom Laurer brought in West Memphis big man Sid (Eudy) Vicious to portray. In one notable situation, WCBI newscaster and future

Bruno Laurer appears at Championship Wrestling's "Tribute to Downtown Bruno" on Friday, July 26, 2019, in Crenshaw, approximately thirty-five miles from Bruno's adopted hometown of Walls. *Tia Howell.*

Columbus mayor Jeffrey Rupp was interviewing Bruno and Humongous when Rupp said something that angered Humongous, leading to the big man pinning Rupp against the wall and choking him. A short feud came from this, as Rupp managed Humongous's opponent one night. Rupp eventually even stepped in the ring himself, teaming with Bill Dundee against Bruno and Humongous at Columbus' Lavender Coliseum.

Bruno and Sid enjoyed considerable success in CCW, but Bruno left when David Woods purchased the territory. Woods had fired Robert Fuller as booker to bring in Eddie Gilbert and Paul E. Dangerously. Afterward, Bruno worked for booker Jerry Stubbs and the IWF in Louisiana, where he managed Sika and others. He soon went back to Continental, which had begun calling itself the Continental Wrestling Federation. In his second stint with the company, Bruno managed the tag team of Jimmy Golden and Brian Lee, as well as a young Cactus Jack. He even held the Southeast United States Junior Heavyweight Title for a few months near the end of 1989. After seeing the territory's end in sight, Bruno left again, eventually returning to Memphis.

In the recently renamed USWA, Bruno managed veteran Phil Hickerson to the Heavyweight Title with a win over Jimmy Valiant, and later managed Jeff Gaylord and Brian Lee. Around that time, he served a forty-five-day sentence in jail for reckless driving. After serving his sentence, Bruno purchased a two-acre piece of land in DeSoto County, Mississippi, in the town of Walls. He got his job back with USWA but soon stopped managing to work in the office and referee for the company after a disagreement with then-booker Eric Embry. In 1991, Sid contacted Bruno about a managerial opening with the WWF, where Sid himself was about to begin wrestling.

Bruno impressed Vince McMahon and others with his quick wit in the Worcester, Massachusetts tryout interview and began working with the company as Harvey Wippleman. His first clients included Sid, Warlord and "Big Bully" Busick, the latter two of whom were very nondescript. Sid was receiving a major push in the company but left in 1992 after being unable to cope with his success. By that time, Bruno began to enjoy the greatest prosperity of his career to that point and moved a small trailer onto the property he purchased in Walls. After Sid's departure, Bruno managed fellow Northwest Mississippian Kamala in a fairly successful run. He feuded with The Undertaker, The Ultimate Warrior and others. After Bruno spent a year with Kamala, the "Ugandan Giant" was turned babyface, with Slick replacing Laurer as his manager. Bruno managed Kamala's former handler Kim Chee in a few matches but would soon be again without a client.

In early 1993, Bruno was paired with the eight-plus-foot-tall Giant Gonzalez. While appearing with Gonzalez on *Live with Regis and Kathie Lee*, Bruno promoted his adopted hometown of Walls while demeaning New York City. Gonzalez mainly feuded with The Undertaker before returning home to his native Argentina after *SummerSlam 1993*. Between 1993 and 1995, Bruno managed Mr. Hughes, Well Dunn, Adam Bomb and Kwang the Ninja, none of whom had major success. On July 4, 1994, Bruno was asleep in the passenger seat of a vehicle driven by Gorilla Monsoon's son, WWF referee Joey Marella. Marella fell asleep behind the wheel and met his death after colliding with a tree. This event had a profound effect on Bruno, though he returned to work after only three weeks. Throughout 1994, he had an ongoing feud with ring announcer Howard Finkel. The feud ended in January 1995, when the two men battled in a Tuxedo Match on *Monday Night Raw*, which Finkel won.

The last wrestler Bruno managed full-time in WWF was Bertha Faye, a large Canadian lady wrestler who played Harvey's onscreen girlfriend. Faye had been a powerful presence in Japan for over a decade under the name Rhonda "Monster Ripper" Sing. She battled Alundra Blayze for the WWF Women's Championship for about six months in 1995, winning the belt at that year's *SummerSlam* before losing it a few months later. After Faye left the company later that year, Bruno's managerial career in the WWF was mostly over. In 1996, he worked as a part-time referee before helping produce interview segments for the company. Not enjoying that work, Bruno carved out a niche for himself, doing the extra things needed to make the show run efficiently and running errands for the McMahons and other high-level WWF/E executives and talents. He called himself the company's "lead concierge" while working in this capacity. He also managed in Randy Hales's Power Pro Wrestling, the first official developmental territory for the WWF, between 1998 and 1999.

In 2000, at the height of the Attitude era, Bruno was placed in gimmick with Mark Henry and elderly women wrestlers Mae Young and The Fabulous Moolah. He played Moolah's love interest and accompanied her to the ring for some of her matches, which were mostly comical at this stage in her career. Around that time, Harvey was asked to dress in drag and win the WWF Women's Title from The Kat, which he did, before dropping the title to Jacqueline the next night. On April 1, 2001, Bruno made his final managerial appearance with the WWF, accompanying Kamala and Kim Chee to the ring for the Gimmick Battle Royal. As of 2021, Bruno continued to work for the WWE in the same backstage role. He also appeared on a couple of nostalgia-themed *Raw* episodes in recent years. He makes regular appearances on independent shows throughout the South, such as *EPW Wrestling*, *VIP Championship Wrestling* and others. In 2000, Bruno married Gail Lundy, and they have two children together. On June 8, 2021, Laurer was elected to a four-year term on the board of alderman in his adopted hometown of Walls.

One friendship that proved valuable was that between Laurer and Rocky Johnson. Laurer met Johnson while working in Hawaii. When Rocky came into CWA, he and Bruno became roommates and good friends. When Rocky's teenage son Dewey came to stay with his dad, he and Bruno hit it off immediately. The underaged Dewey enjoyed the opportunities he had to practice his driving skills, as he often taxied an intoxicated Laurer around the Nashville area. Twenty-four-year-old Dewey, now going by his real name, Dwayne, was brought in for a tryout for the WWF in 1996 and assigned to USWA to gain experience. He briefly stayed in Bruno's home in Walls before moving to an apartment in Memphis. Dwayne, famously known as The Rock, would not forget Bruno's graciousness and friendship, purchasing a brand-new Ford F-150 for him in 2021 as repayment. Bruno is portrayed on the NBC series *Young Rock* and even made a cameo on the show.

11

HENRY HARRELL

enry Winford Harrell was born on February 1, 1922, in Tillman, Mississippi. Besides being a wrestler, Harrell was a World War II veteran and worked for the Illinois Central Railroad in his early life. Henry and his wife, Lucy, had two daughters, Theresa and Mary. By 1944, Harrell had made his wrestling debut and was working around Mississippi and Louisiana.

Harrell eventually wrestled throughout the Southeast and Midwest, enjoying the most success in the late 1940s and early '50s. He was a multiple-time World Light Heavyweight Champion, a former NWA Southern Junior Heavyweight Champion, a World Junior Heavyweight Champion, a Mississippi Heavyweight Champion and a Louisiana Light Heavyweight Champion. He also held the Southern Tag Team Titles with six different partners: Charlie Laye, Pat Newman, Jack Steel, Eddie Gossett (Graham), Buddy Knox and Rex Mobley.

Perhaps Harrell's most memorable moment in professional wrestling occurred on July 24, 1952, in Chattanooga, Tennessee. Harrell, the reigning Southern Junior Heavyweight Champion, was facing World Junior Heavyweight Champion Danny McShain. In the match, McShain was scheduled to get the win, but Harrell was uncooperative. He ended up winning the match when McShain was counted out in the first fall and disqualified in the second. Roy Welch was angered at Harrell's rogue actions and sent his brother Herb into the ring the next night to take Harrell's Southern Title in a shoot, or real fight. Many believed that Welch's business partner, Nick Gulas, put Harrell up to this. Though he continued to work

Henry Harrell. *Gil Culkin.*

for NWA promoters, he was moved down the card and never held another title again. This led to the decision being made that a title could not change hands on a disqualification or count out, though that was not officially a rule until a year later.

Harrell continued wrestling until at least 1957, spending his last few years often working as The Cavalier. After wrestling, Harrell ran several different businesses, such as Ace Amusement Company, Holiday Ice, Wimpy's, P.J.'s and Holiday Beverage. He died from heart failure on June 18, 2000, and was interred at Cedar Hill Cemetery in Vicksburg.

JEAN ANTONE

L ittle Miss Dynamite" Jean Antone was born on July 5, 1943, in Laurel and attended Glade High School. Her in-ring career lasted from 1961 to 1984. She trained in Ella Wladek's Florida backyard. For most of her career, the four-foot, eleven-inch Antone was based out of Bob Geigel's Kansas City office. Unlike most female wrestlers of the time, her career was not controlled by The Fabulous Moolah. Antone's most frequent adversary in the ring was Betty Nicoli. The two faced each other more than four hundred times. Antone also wrestled briefly as Florence Gidget.

Antone was a three-time NWA Central States Women's Champion and a two-time NWA United States Women's Champion. She also won the World Women's Wrestling Association Singles Title and two WWWA Tag Team Titles with Sandy Parker when working for All-Japan Pro Wrestling. She wrestled throughout the United States, Canada and Japan. Antone notably competed in the Gulf Coast region of the Magnolia State.

Antone married Billy Joe McClain in the ring in Laurel on November 6, 1961. They had two daughters together. After retiring from wrestling, she worked at a sewing factory and, later, a convenience store. On August 4, 2016, Antone passed away at the age of seventy-eight.

JIMMY HART

J immy Hart was born on January 1, 1944, in Jackson, Mississippi. After his parents divorced, Jimmy lived with his mother, Sadie, in Memphis. In 1963, while still in high school, Jimmy became a singer in a local band, The Gents, which soon changed its name to The Gentrys. The band's most popular song, "Keep on Dancing," reached no. 4 on Billboard's Hot 100 Chart in 1965, earning the group a deal with MGM. The original lineup recorded two full-length albums and toured extensively, but they were unable to chart higher than no. 50 again. After everyone but Jimmy left the band, he recruited new members and signed a deal with the resurging Sun Records. They had a few more top 100 hits before deciding to set up with a residency at Memphis' Ramada Inn. While hanging out at Sun Studios one day, Hart met Jerry Lawler, who had come to record a few songs. Jimmy ended up singing harmony on Lawler's songs, and the two became friends. Often, on the way home from Tupelo on Friday nights, many of the wrestlers would stop by to hear Jimmy and The Gentrys at the Ramada on Lamar Avenue.

Lawler invited Hart to help promote wrestling shows in his free time. After Lawler had been absent from the ring for a while after losing a "loser leaves town" match to "Handsome" Jimmy Valiant, he asked Hart to appear on TV, setting up a Jerry Lawler / Gentrys concert at the Mid-South Coliseum in Memphis, ostensibly as a send-off for Lawler to go chase his dreams of pop stardom. What this actually did was allow the Lawler-Valiant feud to be resumed, when Valiant broke a guitar over Lawler's head during the performance. Seeking revenge was a way for Lawler to resume in-ring action without devaluing the earlier match. Hart was soon on the payroll, handling promotions and doing some ring announcing and anything else the company needed.

Before long, Hart was serving as Lawler's manager. He helped Lawler turn heel and defeat Bill Dundee in 1978. Two days after his managerial debut, Hart wrestled his first match, defeating "jobber" Pat Hutchinson after interference from Lawler. Hart managed Lawler until February 1980, when Lawler broke his foot in a game of football with friends.

A young Jimmy Hart. *Kathy Hinds Moore.*

Uncertain of Lawler's future, Hart was made the focus of CWA, bringing in numerous heels to battle babyfaces like Bill Dundee and Jimmy Valiant. When Lawler returned from his injury around a year later, he feuded with Hart and his stable of wrestlers, The First Family. This lasted for the next several years.

Hart actually won the Southern Heavyweight Title from Lawler in 1981, thanks to help from First Family members Kevin Sullivan and Wayne Ferris, who were serving as special guest referees, and Gypsy Joe. Lawler had one hand tied behind his back in the match. In late 1981, Hart got another of his only victories, defeating current Itawamba County resident Dennis Upton after interference from Ali Hassan. According to Lance Russell, Hart had substituted for his stable member Sweet Brown Sugar in the match, allowing Sugar to take the night off. Some other wrestlers Hart managed during his time in Memphis were Kamala, "Macho Man" Randy Savage, Rick Rude, The Iron Sheik, Jim Neidhart, Austin Idol, The New York Dolls, Ox Baker, Tommy Rich, Eddie Gilbert, Koko B. Ware, King Kong Bundy, Phil Hickerson, The Original Midnight Express, The Bruise Brothers, Masao Ito, The Nightmares and Bugsy McGraw. Hart even managed and helped train actor Andy Kaufman when he was brought to Memphis for his famous feud with Jerry Lawler. In his time in Memphis, Hart managed his wrestlers to thirty-five championships.

In 1985, Hart left Memphis for the WWF, arriving just prior to the first *WrestleMania*. He made his first appearance at that event, managing his old client King Kong Bundy and then Intercontinental Champion Greg "The Hammer" Valentine. In his early years in WWF, he also managed The Hart Foundation, The Honky Tonk Man, Brutus "The Barber" Beefcake, The

Missing Link, The Funks and Adrian Adonis. Hart also helped produce music for the promotion. He provided a song for *The Wrestling Album* and composed themes for wrestlers such as Shawn Michaels and The Hart Foundation. He continued to participate in the musical side of wrestling during his time in WCW.

After The Hart Foundation fired Jimmy as their manager, he began a feud with the team that lasted several years, bringing several teams in to face them. Against The Hart Foundation, he managed the Fabulous Rougeau Brothers, Demolition, Rhythm and Blues and, later, The Nasty Boys. Hart also managed Dino Bravo, The Natural Disasters and Money Inc. before turning face and aligning with Hulk Hogan in his feud against Yokozuna. Hogan took the World Championship belt from Yoko in twenty-two seconds at *WrestleMania IX* before losing it back to him at that year's *King of the Ring* pay-per-view show. This would be the last match Hart or Hogan would be involved in for WWF for nine years.

Hogan originally left WWF to pursue acting, and Hart served as his personal assistant. When Hogan was filming the television series *Thunder in Paradise*, Hart was given a recurring role and cowrote several songs for the series. Around this time, Hogan met Eric Bischoff, who was in charge of WCW at the time. Bischoff offered Hogan a massive contract, which Hogan accepted. He defeated WCW World Champion Ric Flair in his debut for the company at 1994's *Bash at the Beach* pay-per-view event. Hart, "The Mouth of the South," also served as Hogan's manager there. He accompanied Hogan as he feuded with Flair, The Butcher, Vader and the Kevin Sullivan–led supernatural stable called The Dungeon of Doom. At *Halloween Havoc 1995*, Hart turned on Hogan and aligned with The Dungeon and young wrestler The Giant.

After turning heel, Hart managed The Giant in his WCW World Heavyweight Title reign, as well as Dungeon members "Taskmaster" Kevin Sullivan, Lex Luger, One Man Gang, Big Bubba Rogers, Hugh Morrus, The Faces of Fear, Maxx, Braun the Leprechaun and others. When Hogan turned heel himself and aligned with The New World Order, the Dungeon was pushed down the card. By 1997, many wrestlers in the group aligned with the NWO, leading to The Dungeon's demise. From 1997 through 1999, Hart resurrected his First Family stable, but injuries and WCW's lack of direction led to its failure. Hart worked extensively behind the scenes in the late '90s and into 2001, booking the *WCW Saturday Night* shows each week and composing many wrestlers' themes. When WWF purchased WCW, Hart was not retained.

He had a few stints in NWA TNA and even worked backstage for the company between 2010 and 2011. The WWE inducted him into its Hall of Fame in 2005, and he began working for them in an ambassador-type role in 2011. He continues to appear at wrestling and pop culture conventions and other events around the world. He still occasionally appears on WWE programming and at independent wrestling events, including many in Mississippi. "The Mouth of the South" has made a huge mark in the world of professional wrestling.

14

KAMALA

James Harris was born on May 28, 1950, in Senatobia to sharecropper parents. He began wrestling in 1978 with George and Gil Culkin's International Championship Wrestling, where he worked as Sugar Bear Harris and Ugly Bear Harris, managed by Percy Pringle. He wrestled all over the South and Midwest in his early career, even holding the United States Tag Team Titles with Oki Shikina in 1979 and the Southeastern Heavyweight Title in 1980. He wrestled in Germany and England, adopting the moniker "The Mississippi Mauler" in 1981. He began painting his face while working as this gimmick.

When he returned from England, he went to work in Memphis' CWA, where he and Jerry Lawler created the Kamala, "The Ugandan Giant" character. Many people criticize him for portraying this gimmick that many consider racist, but he said he had fun with the gimmick and meant nothing negative. With this persona, the nearly-four-hundred-pound Harris's face and chest were painted with mock tribal designs, he wore a long cheetah print loincloth, wrestled in bare feet and often carried a tribal mask and spear to the ring. Early on, he briefly held the Southern Heavyweight Title, defeating Lawler for the belt. In 1982, Kamala was briefly turned babyface after being attacked by Plowboy Frazier, who was dressed as Kamala and called himself "Kamala #2." After his initial run with CWA, Kamala began appearing all over the territories. In his first several years as Kamala, he wrestled for Mid-South, Florida, Georgia, Dallas, Kansas City, St. Louis, Jim Crockett Promotions and the AWA

Jake "The Snake" Roberts (*left*) and Kamala (*right*). *Kenny Valiant.*

before starting in the WWF in July 1984. Kamala claimed to have enjoyed working Mid-South the most, and it was there that he said he made the most money. While working there, he began feuding with Andre the Giant, a conflict that traveled across the country.

After his first stint in the WWF, Harris wrestled in Canada and Puerto Rico and even toured with All-Japan Pro Wrestling as Giant Kimala #1. In August 1986, he returned to the WWF, where he stayed over a year, often working world title main events against Hulk Hogan. After not feeling he was being compensated fairly, Kamala left the WWF again in September 1987. After his second WWF run, Kamala worked for WCCW and CWA and made appearances in Japan and Mexico, as well as at independent promotions throughout the United States. Between 1991 and 1992, he worked for the renamed USWA, feuding with Lawler and Koko B. Ware and holding the USWA World Heavyweight Title three times.

In April 1992, he made a third return to the WWF, feuding with The Ultimate Warrior and The Undertaker, but he left in July 1993 after an ill-fated face turn. He continued to feel underpaid during this run with the WWF. After leaving, he continued to work overseas and in independent promotions in the states. Kamala owned his own eighteen-wheeler and spent much of his time away from the ring making deliveries with the truck. In

June 1995, Kamala was brought into WCW by his old friend Hulk Hogan. He worked as a member of The Dungeon of Doom, briefly feuding with Hogan and Hacksaw Jim Duggan before exiting the company in September after participating in the War Games match at WCW's *Fall Brawl* event. This was Kamala's last major run.

He appeared in the Gimmick Battle Royal at *WrestleMania 17* in 2001 and made occasional appearances for the company throughout the early 2000s, notably facing Randy Orton and Umaga. Throughout the 2000s, he wrestled in numerous independent organizations and toured Japan several times with IWA Japan before retiring from the ring in 2010. In the early 2010s, he had both of his legs amputated because of diabetes. He died on August 9, 2020, due to COVID-19.

15

MARKO STUNT

"M r. Fun-Size" Marko Stunt, whose real name is Noah Nelms, was born on July 30, 1996, in Paragould, Arkansas. His father was a Southern Baptist pastor and missionary. Marko and his family moved around a lot when he was younger, living all over the northern portion of Mississippi, as well as in Costa Rica and Nicaragua, before settling in Olive Branch. In 2015, Marko graduated from Lewisburg High School. In 2014, at age seventeen, Stunt began attending wrestling school with a group of friends, including notable indie worker Walker Hayes, after talking to some local wrestlers at an independent show. After Marko fell out with his original trainer, veteran Mississippi wrestler Motley Cruz schooled him in the mat game.

In January 2015, he had his first match. His diminutive size, along with his high-flying ability, retro style and natural charisma, separated Stunt from the wrestling masses. At five feet, two inches tall and weighing under 150 pounds, Stunt has a considerable size disadvantage against most of his opponents. By 2018, he worked on independent shows around Tennessee and Mississippi, such as Total Wrestling Explosion and Pro Wrestling EGO, for Cape Championship Wrestling, based in Cape Girardeau, Missouri; Anarchy Championship Wrestling in Austin, Texas; and IWA Mid-South. In April, he won his first title, the CCW Tag Team Championship, with Mikey McFinnegan. In July, he won the CCW Heavyweight Title in a three-way match over Flip Gordon and fellow Mississippian Jacksyn Crowley, who was the champion going into the match. Stunt feuded with Crowley and Austin Lane in that promotion.

Marko Stunt at EPW Arena in Booneville, Mississippi. *Star Shots by Christy; owner, Christy Harville.*

On August 4, Stunt won the Scenic City Invitational Futures Showcase Tournament. His star was on the rise, and he received his first big break on August 17, on *SummerSlam Weekend* in New York, when he first appeared for Game Changer Wrestling (GCW). Stunt answered Kyle the Beast's open challenge. Even in defeat, this appearance caught the attention of Cody Rhodes, who put Stunt in the battle royal at *All In*, the pay-per-view event that was the forerunner to All Elite Wrestling. After this, Marko began appearing all over the country, winning the Southern Underground Pro Bonestorm Title on September 23 and gaining wins over wrestlers like Maxwell Jacob Friedman, Swoggle and PCO (Carl Ouellet. On November 16, at a GCW event in Los Angeles, California, Stunt broke his leg while taking a Canadian Destroyer. He returned on April 5, 2019, at another GCW event, winning over Joey Janela.

When AEW held its first event on May 25, Stunt participated again in the battle royal. He officially signed with the company in July and was placed in The Jurassic Express with Luchasaurus and Jungle Boy. The group was among the top merchandise sellers in AEW's earliest days. Stunt was most often used to put over other workers in matches, with his only wins in the company coming over lower-tier talent. While with the company, Marko very briefly held The Dramatic Dream Team Iron Man Heavymetalweight Title and the Revolution Eastern Wrestling Pakistani 24/7 Title, both titles with 24/7 rules. He won the titles from Jungle Boy on November 12 and lost them the same night to female wrestler Dr. Britt Baker. During his time with AEW, he worked on shows intermittently for GCW, CCW, Black Label Pro, Booneville-based EPW Wrestling and others. In August 2021, Stunt defeated Brandon Barbwire to win his second CCW Heavyweight Title. His AEW contract ended in May 2022 and was not renewed. Stunt continues to appear on independent shows across the country and was named the executive vice-president and co-booker of CCW. Marko's younger brother Logan Stunt is also an accomplished wrestler. Besides wrestling, Marko Stunt is a gifted singer and guitar player.

16

MAX PALMER

Max Edmund Palmer was born on November 2, 1927, in Mississippi. He would grow to be one of the tallest men in the world. By 1930, his family owned a small cotton farm in Quitman County in the Delta. When Max was six, his father passed away from an alcohol-related illness. His bootlegger uncles then took an active role in Max's life, which he claimed led to his alcohol addiction. He turned to this vice at an early age when others ridiculed him for looking different. Max was the only member of his family above average height. He was examined by a slew of doctors, but none were able to find the cause of his tremendous growth.

Max attended high school at Walnut Consolidated School in Vance, Mississippi. By this time, he had grown to seven feet, two inches tall, and was the starting center on the school's basketball team. Harold Lusk, who also played on the Walnut High School team, recalled that Palmer was not a great athlete but still took over games. According to him, Max did not play defense at all. Instead, he sat under the opponent's basket and waited for his teammates to pass him the ball. He then simply dropped the ball into the hoop. Lusk remembered that Sledge High School tried defending Palmer by stacking one player on another's shoulders. This strategy was unsuccessful, because Palmer easily outmaneuvered the stacked duo, even with his extremely limited speed. In 1947, Palmer set the Mississippi state record for most points in a high school basketball game by a single player, with 78. This scoring barrage came in a 104–8 win over Darling High, a game Max played in only through the third quarter. Palmer had grown to seven feet, seven inches, at the time of his record-setting performance. After high school, Palmer traveled to play professional basketball for the Rochester Royals. He lasted only a few games, because coaches were dissatisfied with his lack of effort in rebounding, likely due to his perpetual drunkenness at that time.

After his failed attempt at pro basketball, Palmer set his sights on Hollywood. He made two movies, *Killer Ape* and *Invaders from Mars*, and appeared on television programs like *The Martin and Lewis Show*. According to his stepson Shane, Max was also considered to play Lurch in *The Addams Family*. During this time, Max began to dabble in heavy drug use. He blamed this and his continued alcoholism for cutting his acting career short.

He then moved to Salt Lake City, Utah, and began a seven-year foray into professional wrestling. He toured throughout the United States and Canada, billed as "Paul Bunyan" at times and his given name at others. At various times during his Hollywood and wrestling days, his height was billed anywhere from seven feet, seven inches, to eight feet, six inches. He weighed between 375 and 400 pounds. He wrestled Bobo Brazil, Dick the Bruiser, Gene Kiniski, Verne Gagne, Mario Galento, The Crusher, Angelo Poffo and "Whipper" Billy Watson, among many others. He was often placed in handicap matches against two or more smaller men. The move

Poster for Crusade featuring Max Palmer. *Wikimedia Commons.*

Max most often relied on was the bear hug. Though Max's lack of athleticism suggests that he was not a technically gifted wrestler, this did not stop people from paying to see him. He was one of the most popular attractions in professional wrestling of the day, paving the way for big men like Andre the Giant, The Big Show and The Great Khali to have successful careers inside the ring. Max's wife, Betty, once said that he left wrestling because he did not take the promoter's command to lose a match. Palmer's son says that his father disliked always playing a heel.

After his wrestling career, the effects of Max's addictions began to peak. He had recently moved to Oklahoma to work as a bartender when Max was hospitalized for severe stomach ulcers. While hospitalized, a pastor from a local church visited him and led him to reexamine his life. Max embraced Christianity not long after his recovery, never drinking alcohol or abusing drugs again. He even overcame chain-smoking. Six months after accepting his new faith, he began touring the nation as an evangelist, where he was given the nickname "Goliath for Christ." He met his future wife, Betty Pinnell, while making a preaching appearance at a church in Decatur, Illinois, in 1974. Within seven months, the two were wed.

The marriage was not popular with Betty's family. She was twenty-two years younger than Max, three feet shorter and weighed almost three hundred pounds less. The couple settled in Arnold, Missouri, with Pinnell's two children from a previous relationship. The marriage and children were the answer to eleven years of prayer from Palmer, according to his wife.

Palmer died on May 7, 1984, at St. Anthony's Medical Center in St. Louis, Missouri, of congestive heart failure. He was in the hospital at the time for chronic swelling in his left leg. Palmer's body was laid to rest in Cary Springs Cemetery near Pontotoc, where his mother is buried. He was measured at eight feet, two inches tall, and weighed 475 pounds at the time of his death.

17

PLOWBOY FRAZIER / UNCLE ELMER

Stanley Cooper Frazier was born in Philadelphia on August 16, 1937. In his early life, he served in the U.S. Navy in Korea, played semipro football and was a chef aboard a merchant marine vessel. He made his in-ring debut in 1960, wrestling around the South under many names, including Stan/Stanley Frazier, Giant Frazier, Tiny Frazier, The Country Plowboy, Country Boy, Ed Younger, Big Tex, Pascagoula Plowboy, Mississippi Plowboy, Texas Plowboy, Playboy Frazier, Cowboy Frazier, Kamala #2, A-Team #2, the Giant Rebel, The Lone Ranger and The Giant Hillbilly. His most notable personas were Plowboy Frazier around the Southeast, Uncle Elmer in the WWF and The Convict in Hawaii and Japan. He first used this latter moniker during his time with the WWF.

In 1967, the seven-foot, four-hundred-pound wrestler was billed as the Southern Heavyweight Champion. He spent much of his career wrestling for Nick Gulas and Roy Welch or Jerry Jarrett in the Memphis area, though he traveled throughout the United States, Canada and Japan. He held multiple tag team titles over the years, including the NWA World Tag Team, Southern Tag Team, NWA National Tag Team and AWA Southern Tag Team Titles. His partners for these championship runs included Lawler, Ted DiBiase, Dennis Hall, Cousin Junior and Terry Sawyer.

Perhaps, he is most remembered for marrying his wife, Joyce, on WWF's *Saturday Night's Main Event* on NBC. He was a member of the hillbilly faction with Hillbilly Jim, Cousin Luke and Cousin Junior. He wrestled in a match at *WrestleMania II*, losing to Adrian Adonis. After his WWF run, Frazier held the CWA Super Heavyweight Title twice.

Plowboy Frazier (*left*) and Ken "The Dream" Rose. Rose, going by the name Cousin Kenny, teamed with Frazier. *Kenny Valiant.*

Frazier was a very enterprising individual. He operated several of his own wrestling promotions, partnering with Miriam Springfield at times, and he trained wrestlers like Bob Holly and Koko B. Ware. He owned a shoe store and sold fake Rolexes. He also appeared in a few movies, once playing the part of Bigfoot. He died on July 5, 1992, of kidney failure resulting from his weight and diabetic condition. He was laid to rest in Biloxi National Cemetery.

BIBLIOGRAPHY

Anderson, H. Allen. "Dutch Mantell." Texas State Historical Association. Updated November 30, 2019. https://www.tshaonline.org.

Ashley's Adventures. "Elvis and Penny Banner." YouTube, April 24, 2020. 3:45. https://www.youtube.com/watch?v=dd_gChd249g&vl=en.

Askeland, Kevin. "Highest Single-Game Boys High School Basketball Totals from Each Year Since 1906." MaxPreps. March 5, 2020. https://www.maxpreps.com.

Baker, Lee. "Local Promoter Sees Nothing of Rebirth." *Clarion-Ledger*, July 22, 1985.

Barry, Joseph P. "A Card," letter. *Pensacola News*, February 22, 1891.

Beekman, Scott M. *Ringside: A History of Professional Wrestling in America.* Waterbury, CT: Praeger, 2006.

Beveridge, Lici. "Brett DiBiase, Former DHS Official, Pleads Guilty to Federal Conspiracy Charge. *Clarion Ledger*, March 2, 2023.

Biloxi (MS) Daily Herald. "Athletic Promoter Given Jail Term at Hattiesburg." May 10, 1930.

———. "Bilbo Gives His Reasons." March 30, 1928.

———. "Colored Women Set to Wrestle in Legion Arena." August 27, 1952.

———. "Dempsey, Schmeling to Be Tried Before Mississippi Group." April 7, 1931.

———. "Farrington of Butte Threw Hackenschmidt in 58 Minutes." December 19, 1911.

————. "Feminine Mat Stars to Vie in Pascagoula." June 15, 1939.

————. "James Victor in Wrestling Contest." August 24, 1911.

————. "Jap Wrestler Wins." May 1, 1931.

————. "Lady Wrestlers Featured in Mat Program Friday." August 30, 1956.

————. "New 145-Pound Champ Crowned in Keesler Ring." November 18, 1944.

————. "Pierce Again in Show Business." June 18, 1908.

————. "Third Tallest Man in the World to Be Buried in Hometown of Pontotoc." May 9, 1984.

————. "Thousands Cheer Athletes in Tournament at Station." November 21, 1918.

————. "Three Boxing Bouts and Mat Scrap on Card." October 1, 1938.

————. "To Make More Room for Fans." February 15, 1926.

————. "Velam Jordaan Captures Main Wrestling Event." November 8, 1945.

————. "Women Occupy Feature Spot on Mat Program." September 3, 1946.

————. "Women Wrestlers to Vie Tonight in Card Opener." August 23, 1944.

————. "Wrestler Dies of Heart Attack in Ring at Corinth." May 15, 1937.

————. "Wrestling," advertisement. September 4, 1961.

————. "Wrestling Tourney Takes Place Saturday." August 5, 1992.

Bischoff, Eric, and Conrad Thompson. "Uncensored 1995." *83 Weeks.* Podcast. October 27, 2022. https://podcasts.apple.com/us/podcast/episode-46-uncensored-95/id1137115592?i=1000431524242.

Blaylock, Jimmy. Interview with author. Tuesday, November 7, 2022.

————. "WCBI Reporter Jeffrey Rupp Pisses Off Lord Humongous." YouTube. 3:35. www.youtube.com.

Brandon (MS) News. "The Entertainment Given Last Friday Was Successful." September 1, 1910.

Brisco, Gerald, and John "Bradshaw" Layfield. Interview with Ron Fuller. *Stories with Brisco and Bradshaw.* Podcast. October 27, 2022. https://podcasts.apple.com/us/podcast/special-guest-ron-fuller/id1557108431i=1000584077678.

Brownsville (TX) Herald. "Fast Bouts Are Billed." February 4, 1932.

Bryan County, Oklahoma. Marriage Certificate 131 (1933). Curtis-Strickland, Decatur, OK. Ancestry.com. https://www.ancestrylibrary.com.

Burnham, Bubba. "Wrestling Returns to Delta Jubilee." *Clarksdale (MS) Press Register*, March 31, 2000.

Buser, Lawrence. "Death Fells Giant Who Bested Booze, Stood Tall for God." *Commercial Appeal* (Memphis, TN), May 11, 1984.

Caldwell, Stan. "NWA Bringing Big-Time Wrestling to USM." *Hattiesburg (MS) American*, April 8, 1987.

Calloway. "YouTube Terry Gordy vs. Mr. Olympia," Wrestling Classics message board, August 23, 2010. http://wrestlingclassics.com.

Carman, Carol Springfield. Interview with author, November 22, 2022.

Carr, Cathi. "Friday Night Wrestling Card Includes Former USM Player Wren." *Hattiesburg (MS) American*, December 1988.

C.C. Milani from NY. "Edumacate Me on NWF Heritage Championship Wrestling." Wrestling Classics message board, March 27, 2021. http://wrestlingclassics.com.

Charlotte (NC) News. "Walt Evans Coming Here December 21." December 9, 1910.

Charting the Territories Presents the ICW/AWA Championship Wrestling (George & Gil Culkin-Mississippi) Almanac (October 1977–August 1979). Chartingtheterritories.com, 2020.

Choctaw Plaindealer (Ackerman, MS). "Wrestling Match!" July 1, 1921.

Cincinnati (OH) Post. "Eight Feet, Two Inches: But Can He Wrestle?" July 9, 1978.

Clarion (Jackson, MS). "An Athletic Entertainment Is Scheduled for Robinson's Opera House Tonight." December 10, 1884.

Clarion-Ledger (Jackson, MS). "Ali Pasha Listed for Local Match." March 6, 1955.

———. "Attorney General Rules Wrestling/Boxing Illegal." November 10, 1927.

———. "Baron Leoni to Wrestle Here Friday." March 13, 1955.

———. "Big Program Set by Heavyweights." November 14, 1937.

———. "Blimp All Set for Big Fight." April 7, 1938.

———. "City News." June 18, 1926.

———. "Col. H.J. Landry Dies in Memphis." January 4, 1955.

———. "Columbus to See Real Wrestling Bout." January 8, 1926.

———. "Corsica Brothers See First Action Here Tonight at City Auditorium." June 4, 1957.

———. "Curtis Makes Mince-Meat of Texas Wrestler." May 27, 1956.

———. "Curtis Pummels Steddum's Head." May 27, 1956.

———. "Dermitroff Wins." January 6, 1926.

———. "Fair's Second Day Wonderful Success Great Crowds Out." October 20, 1926.

———. "Former Champion in Jackson Ring." October 27, 1938.

———. "Friday Night." August 29, 1956.

———. "Heavyweights Set for Tilts Tonight." October 21, 1937.

———. "Henry Wilford Harrel," obituary. February 2, 1988.

———. "Jackson Becomes Center of Sports for Wide Area and All Receive Support." November 5, 1926.

———. "Legion Wrestlers Meet Here Tonight." April 22, 1932.

———. "The Legislature: In the House." April 6, 1928.

———. "Local Wrestlers to Get Challenge from Circus Champ." October 25, 1923.

———. "Ludwig Defeats Welch in Match." April 12, 1936.

———. "Mantell to Meet Alli Hassan Here." January 9, 1927.

———. "McComb Sticks to No Fight Policy." September 8, 1927.

———. "Meridian Staging Big Title Match." January 13, 1927.

———. "The Midget Rasslers Are Here and Ready for a Major Romp at City Auditorium Next Friday." April 22, 1951.

———. "On Strangle Card Tonight." December 25, 1937.

———. "Pancho Villa Invites Art Neilson to Whip Curtis Team." April 24, 1959.

———. "Plan Wrestling Bout." August 16, 1925.

———. "The Question of Evolution Will Be Reopened Here at the City Auditorium." February 2, 1950.

———. "Rebel Championship Wrestling," advertisement. May 31, 1963.

———. "Retiring." February 13, 1955.

———. "Romanoff at Tupelo." February 3, 1935.

———. "Romanoff Injured and Champion Wins in Fall from the Ring." February 18, 1927.

———. "Stecher Is Victor in Straight Falls." January 20, 1927.

———. "Team-Match Idea Appeals to Fans." July 5, 1938.

———. "Titled Russian Is to Train Wrestlers." November 29, 1925.

———. "Tuesday Wrestling." June 16, 1956.

———. "TV Announcer." April 15, 1955.

———. "Two Attractions on Wrestling Bill." January 26, 1934.

———. "Victor Kaulfus of Pensacola, Florida, Lightweight Wrestling Champion of the South, Is Here Today." March 18, 1922.

———. "World Class Championship Wrestling," advertisement. March 29, 1987.

———. "World Class Championship Wrestling," advertisement. March 13, 1988.

———. "Wrestlers Set for Exhibition Tonight." December 30, 1925.

———. "Wrestling," advertisement. December 23, 1955.

———. "Wrestling," advertisement. February 11, 1962.

———. "Wrestling," advertisement. September 2, 1965.

———. "Wrestling Match." July 26, 1931.

———. "Wrestling Match Details Complete." November 28, 1925.

Clarke County Tribune (Quitman, MS). "Tri-State Championship Wrestling," advertisement. June 11, 1981.

Clarke, Gerald. *Capote: A Biography*. New York: RosettaBooks, 1988.

Clarksdale (MS) Press Register. "Heritage Championship Wrestling," advertisement. September 30, 1989.

———. "Professional Wrestling," advertisement. January 21, 2022.

———. "Splash Adds Wrestling." April 16, 1993.

———. "Wrestling Is Now Fair Sex Mat Objective." December 20, 1927.

Clayton, Kenny. Interview with author, October 18, 2022.

Cleveland, Rick "No Tall Tale Here: Today's Hotshots Can't Touch Max." *Clarion-Ledger* (Jackson, MS), January 12, 1989.

Columbian-Progress (Columbia, MS). "Veterans of Foreign Wars to Sponsor Wrestling Here Weekly." July 25, 1957.

———. "Wrestling Event Features Columbia Participants." September 27, 2001.

Columbus (MS) Commercial. "Free Exhibition by Athletic Association." April 4, 1905.

Columbus (MS) Dispatch. "Legion Match Is Even Break." August 4, 1920.

———. "Legion Wrestling Match Tomorrow." September 12, 1920.

———. "Local Wrestling Champion." November 12, 1919.

———. "May Get Another Wrestling Match." April 28, 1920.

The Comet (Jackson, MS). "Rolla Ryan Will Be Here Next Friday, and Will Give an Entertainment for One Night Only…" April 10, 1880.

Corrigan, John. "The Untold Stories of 'Heroes of Wrestling.'" The Wrestling Estate, October 10, 2019. www.thewrestlingestate.com.

Culkin, Gil. Interview with author, December 7, 2022.

———. *The Mississippi Wrestling Territory: The Untold Story*. N.p.: self-published, 2012.

Daily Capital News (Jefferson City, MO). "Peter James Dies in Holts Summit." March 11, 1958.

Daily Record-Tribune (Gulfport, MS). "Wrestling Last Night at Pierce's Air Dome." July 16, 1908.

———. "Wrestling Match Tonight at Pierce's Air Dome." July 9, 1908.

————. "Wrestling Tonight at Pierce's Air Dome." July 18, 1908.

Delta Democrat-Times (Greenville, MS). "Fields Brothers to Head Mat Card." March 10, 1955.

————. "5 Men Wrestle Blindfolded Here on Saturday Night." April 4, 1957.

————. "Frank Hurley and Terror on Mat Card." June 13, 1956.

————. "3 New Grapplers on the Greenville Card for Saturday." February 15, 1955.

————. "Woman Wrestles Gator in Arena Here Saturday." May 11, 1954.

————. "Wrestling Matches Set Here." December 7, 1966.

————. "Wrestling Saturday Night," advertisement. May 27, 1955.

Dent, Paxton H. "Just as It Seems." *El Paso (TX) Times*, November 8, 1933.

DiBiase, Ted, with Tom Caiazzo. *Million Dollar Man: Ted DiBiase*. New York: Pocket Books, 2008.

Dinner with the King Podcast. "Jerry Lawler and Elvis Presley Almost Had a Match." YouTube, December 6, 2017. 10:05. https://www.youtube.com/watch?v=NudwnDynEFk.

Doyal, Gregg. "All Voices Need to Be Heard, Let's Listen." *Evansville (IN) Courier & Press*, August 30, 2020.

Duncan, Royal, and Gary Will. *Wrestling Title Histories*. 4th ed. Waterloo, ON: Archeus Communications, 2000.

Dunn, J.A.C. "Wrestling His Way Through College." *Chapel Hill (NC) Weekly*, October 17, 1960.

Dupree, Marcus. Interview with author, November 27, 2022.

East Mississippi Times (Starkville, MS). "The Juvanal Shows." October 24, 1914.

Enterprise-Journal (McComb, MS). "Girls Wrestle Here." September 17, 1956.

————. "Southwestern Championship Wrestling," advertisement. April 11, 1972.

————. "Wrestling," advertisement. March 30, 1979.

————. "Wrestling Brought Here Saturday by Harvey Post." November 18, 1947.

————. "Wrestling Opens Events Center in Tylertown." September 7, 2000.

Enterprise-Tocsin (Indianola, MS). "Fine Crowd at Wrestling Match." December 17, 1925.

————. "Wrestling Is Tonight at 7 P.M., MDCC." December 13, 1990.

Ernst, Ken. "400 Pound Wrestler Is Merchant Marine Chef." *Sun Herald* (Biloxi, MS), February 5, 1972.

Everett, Maria. Interview with author. Facebook Messenger, October 20, 2022. www.facebook.com.

FAM People. "Bruno Laurer." May 19, 2019. https://fampeople.com.

The Famous People. "Ted DiBiase." https://www.thefamouspeople.com.

Find a Grave. "Elbert James 'Jack' Curtis." Accessed November 18, 2022. www.findagrave.com.

Finley, Pat. "Wrestling Match Thursday Night." *Magee (MS) Courier*, February 12, 1987.

Fisher, Kelley. "The Dying Art of Speaking Ceazarnie." Lousiana Folklife. https://www.louisianafolklife.org.

Fisher-Riles Funeral Home. "Jack Curtis, Jr.," obituary. Accessed November 20, 2022. https://www.fisherrilesfuneralhome.com.

Graham, Charlotte. "Wrestling for Souls." *Clarion-Ledger*, September 26, 1998.

Greenberg, Keith Elliot. *Too Sweet: Inside the Indie Wrestling Revolution*. Toronto, ON: ECW Press, 2020.

Greenwood (MS) Commonwealth. "Championship Wrestling," advertisement. June 25, 1986.

———. "Former Professional Wrestler Turns to Politics." September 13, 1984.

———. "High Cotton, 300 Oaks: Fun and Entertainment Delta Style." September 19, 1999.

———. "It's a Man's World So Far as Local Wrestling Heads Are Concerned." February 1, 1938.

———. "Mississippian Heads National Wrestling." September 25, 1931.

———. "Professional Wrestling Due to Come to Greenwood Next Friday." March 7, 1967.

———. "Small Events Adding Up for Leflore County Civic Center." July 11, 1988.

———. "Wrestling," advertisement. August 16, 1956.

———. "Wrestling," advertisement. April 20, 1971.

———. "Wrestling to Be Staged Here." September 28, 1937.

Greer, Jamie. "Jimmy Hart & The First Family: Three Decades of Dominance." Last Word on Sports. August 10, 2022. https://lastwordonsports.com.

Griffin, Lolly. Interview with author, December 8, 2022.

Grimes, Rodney. Interview with author, February 21, 2023.

Hales, Randy. Interview with author. Facebook Messenger, November 10, 2022. www.facebook.com.

————. *Living the Dream: Memphis Wrestling: The Randy Hales Story.* N.p.: self-published, 2020.

Hanna, Raina. "DeSoto Wrestler Noah Nelms Climbs Professional Ladder." *Commercial Appeal* (Memphis, TN), September 16, 2018.

The Hannibal TV. "Honky Tonk Man on Tupelo Concession Stand Brawl." YouTube, February 19, 2015. 5:15. https://www.youtube.com/watch?v=d1Nts53qb8g.

————. "Jerry Jarrett Full Career Shoot Interview 4.5 Hours." YouTube, January 1, 2019. https://youtu.be/ZWGp1EKNdUI.

Hart, Jimmy. *The Mouth of the South: The Jimmy Hart Story.* Toronto, ON: ECW Press, 2004.

Haskins, David. Interview with author, November 22, 2022.

Hattiesburg (MS) American. "All Star Wrestling," advertisement. September 11, 1956.

————. "At Greater Hattiesburg Park," advertisement. April 17, 1951.

————. "Bill Baylis Fatally Injured." November 7, 1973.

————. "Championship Wrestling," advertisement. August 14, 1986.

————. "Colored Wrestling Wednesday Night at Star Theatre." July 17, 1961.

————. "Two Lady Angels Wrestling in Mississippi." June 18, 1957.

————. "VFW to Sponsor Matches Here." May 30, 1941.

————. "Women's Wrestling Champion to Defend Here Next Week." May 5, 1942.

————. "Wrestling," advertisement. October 16, 1951.

————. "Wrestling," advertisement. April 15, 1968.

————. "Wrestling!," advertisement. May 3, 1974.

————. "Wrestling Returns Here Thursday." October 28, 1957.

————. "Wrestling Riles Fans with Morality Plays." March 17, 2004.

Hattiesburg (MS) Daily News. "Big Wrestler Is a Favorite." October 23, 1907.

————. "Big Wrestler Is a Favorite." February 8, 1913.

————. "Great Wrestling Match Hattiesburg, October 26." October 19, 1907.

————. "Wrestling Match at the Auditorium." October 24, 1907.

Hederman, Arnold, "Highlights in Sports." *Clarion-Ledger* (Jackson, MS), December 16, 1950.

Herald and Review (Decatur, IL). "Giant Wrestler Lisowski Boys Win at Lakeview." March 2, 1957.

Hessler, Warner. "Coastin' on Sports." *Biloxi (MS) Daily Herald*, November 3, 1966.

Hobbs, E.T., ed. "Mormon Conference." *The Leader* (Brookhaven, MS), January 18, 1898.

Holt, Aaron. Interview with author, January 4, 2023.

Honolulu (HI) Star-Bulletin. "Newcomers Show in Rassling at the Auditorium." November 3, 1934.

Hornbaker, Tim. "Colonel Harry J. Landry." Legacy of Wrestling. Accessed October 7, 2022. http://www.legacyofwrestling.com.

———. *Death of the Territories: Expansion, Betrayal, and the War that Changed Pro Wrestling Forever.* Toronto, ON: ECW Press, 2018.

———. *Legends of Pro Wrestling: 150 Years of Headlocks, Bodyslams, and Piledrivers.* New York: Sports Publishing, 2016.

———. *National Wrestling Alliance: The Untold Story of the Monopoly that Strangled Pro Wrestling.* Toronto, ON: ECW Press, 2007.

Horton, John. Interview with author. Facebook Messenger, November 20, 2022. www.Facebook.com.

Hunzinger, Erica. "Explanation: Favre, Other Sports Figures in Mississippi Welfare Fraud Case." Fox 11, October 3, 2022. https://fox11online.com.

Internet Movie Database. "Jimmy Hart Biography." https://www.imdb.com.

Jackson (MS) Daily News. "Dairymen Organize." February 17, 1916.

———. "Wrestlers at Grenada." April 6, 1919.

———. "Wrestlers Be Seen in Action Thursday." May 6, 1914.

———. "Wrestling Match Attracting Attention." May 26, 1912.

James, Mark, and Tim Dills. *Memphis Wrestling History: Tennessee Record Book 1960–1972.* N.p.: self-published, 2014.

———. *Memphis Wrestling History: Tennessee Record Book 1973–1979.* N.p.: Self-published, 2014,

Johnston, Erle. "Romanoff's Rasslin' Rodeos Featured Heroes and Vilyuns." *Clarion-Ledger* (Jackson, MS), February 18, 1955.

Jones County News (Ellisville, MS). "Legion Match…," advertisement for American Legion Picnic. July 1, 1920.

Kery, Charlie. "Atta Boy! Sports: News Views Comment." *Delta Democrat-Times*, October 20, 1938.

Klein, Christopher. *Strong Boy: The Life and Times of John L. Sullivan, America's First Sports Hero.* Guilford, CT: Lyons, 2013.

Kreikenbohm, Philip. Cagematch. www.cagematch.net.

Lambert, Jeremy, "Marko Stunt Reveals Plan to Open His Own Promotion in September." Fightful. July 7, 2022. https://www.fightful.com.

LaPrade, Pat. "Promoters Signing Wrestlers Exclusively." Wrestling Classics message board, January 17, 2019. http://wrestlingclassics.com.

Laurel (MS) Ledger. "Y.M.C.A." January 14, 1909.

Laurer, Bruno, with Scott Teal. *Wrestling with the Truth*. Gallatin, TN: Crowbar Press, 2008.

LeBlanc, J.A. "Harvey Wippleman." Online World of Wrestling. Updated January 9, 2019. https://www.onlineworldofwrestling.com.

Linder, Zach. "Inside the Dungeon of Doom: Kevin Sullivan on Wrestling's Wackiest Group." WWE.com. https://www.wwe.com.

Luther, Rex. Interview with author, November 26, 2022.

Magee (MS) Courier. "Sat. Night Wrestling," advertisement. May 23, 1957.

Marshall (TX) News Messenger. "Czechoslovakian Neck Twister and Former Movie Actor Meet on Mat Card Here Wednesday." November 20, 1932.

Martin, Archie H., Jr. "Sports Corner." *Enterprise Journal* (McComb, MS), September 16, 1938.

McClain, Danny. Interview with author, January 2, 2023.

McKay, Doug. "Wrestling Returns to Louisville." *Winston County Journal* (Louisville, MS), February 21, 1990.

———. "Wrestling Returns to Nanih Waiya." *Winston County Journal*, October 21, 1987.

———. "Wrestling to Return." *Winston County Journal*, May 16, 1990.

McKibben, Rusty. "7'8" Man Spreads Word." *Columbia (SC) Record*, September 20, 1971.

Mitchell, Jerry. "Mother, Son Plead Guilty in Fraud Case." *Clarion-Ledger*, April 26, 1990.

Monroe (LA) Morning World. "3 Curtises Wrestler Tues." December 19, 1954.

Mooneyham, Mike. "Sputnik Monroe Helped Break Down Color Barrier in Pro Wrestling." *Post and Courier* (Charleston, SC), November 27, 2020.

National Archives and Records Administration. "World War II Draft Registration Card for Henry Winford Harrel." Ancestry.com. Accessed on January 15, 2022. www.ancestry.com.

Newton (MS) Record. "Wrestling Match," advertisement. August 16, 1956.

O'Hara, Kassondra. "The French Angel." Medium, November 1, 2020. https://medium.com.

Oliver, Greg. "'Little Miss Dynamite' Jean Antone Dies." Slam Wrestling. August 4, 2016. https://slamwrestling.net.

Oliver, Greg, and Jon Waldman, eds. *Slam! Wrestling: Shocking Stories from the Squared Circle*. Toronto, ON: ECW Press, 2009.

Oliver, Greg, and Steven Johnson. *The Pro Wrestling Hall of Fame: The Heels*. Toronto, ON: ECW Press, 2007.

———. *The Pro Wrestling Hall of Fame: The Tag Teams.* Toronto, ON: ECW Press, 2005.

O'Neal, Ed. "Learning from Life: Thomas Randolph Curtis." *Richmond (NC) Observer*, August 9, 2018.

Palmer-Pinnell, Shane. Interview with author. Facebook Messenger, July 19, 2022. www.facebook.com.

Pappas, Thomas N., Jr., "He's Even Tall Enough for Reaching Hollywood Stars." *Memphis (TN) Press-Scimitar,* December 15, 1952.

Parker, Thomas C. "IPWA Championship Wrestling," advertisement. *Clarion-Ledger* (Jackson, MS), March 16, 2006.

PartsUnknown77 From ND. "Not OT:Matt Riviera/MillionaireMatchMaker." Wrestlingclassics.comMessageBoard,March19,2013.http://wrestlingclassics.com/.ubb/ultimatebb.phpubb=get_topic;f=1;t=132304#000011.

Pettus, Gary. "Don't Call It Fake." *Clarion-Ledger*, March 7, 1996.

Poole, Edith. Interview with author. Facebook Messenger, February 21, 2023. www.facebook.com.

Postl, Dylan. "Small Talk with Marko Stunt." YouTube, June 13, 2002. https://youtu.be/H9Gat1aiT18.

Prehn, Paul, *Scientific Methods of Wrestling.* Champaign, IL: Bailey & Himes, Publishers, 1925.

Press and Sun-Bulletin (Binghamton, NY). "Mississippi Town Presents Holiday Aspect at Hanging." August 20, 1920.

Pro Wrestling History. "Information About the National Wrestling Federation." http://www.prowrestlinghistory.com.

Ragland, Lee. "Hulkamania Headlocks 4,500." *Clarion-Ledger*, October 5, 1986.

Ross, Shelly. "Wrestler Signs Contract for Bigfoot Movie Role." *Yazoo Herald* (Yazoo City, MS), December 3, 1978.

Rowland, Tonya. Interview with author. Facebook Messenger, December 17, 2022. www.facebook.com.

Salina (KS) Journal. "Goliath for Christ Holds All Eyes." March 7, 1969.

Sanders, William. "Elva George Culkin." Find a Grave. Created July 2, 2018. https://www.findagrave.com.

Scott County Times (Forest, MS). "Junkyard Dog Killed at Lake." June 4, 1998.

———. "Professional Wrestling," advertisement. August 24, 1966.

Semi-Weekly Leader (Brookhaven, MS). "Cutrer Beats Furr." May 24, 1916.

———. "Furr and Hanson in Return Wrestling Match." November 11, 1922.

———. "Hanson Insists on Return Match with Henry Furr." December 30, 1922.

———. "Henry Furr Again Bests Wrestler Gustave Hanson." November 18, 1922.

———. "Henry Furr a 'Grown in Mississippi' Product." November 24, 1915.

———. "Leo Hackenschmidt, a Professional Wrestler, and J.W. Evans, a Blacksmith, Pulled Off a Good Match Thursday Night at Woodmen Hall." April 4, 1914.

———. "Lincoln County's Field Day." Saturday, April 23, 1910.

———. "Members Named of Athletic Board." April 6, 1928.

———. "Tax Wrestling Bouts." January 21, 1923.

———. "The Wrestling Match a Clean One—Very Interesting and Hardly Contested." March 28, 1914.

———. "Wrestling Match a Disappointment." December 20, 1922.

Shannon, Jake. *Say Uncle!: Catch-as-Catch-Can Wrestling and the Roots of Ultimate Fighting, Pro Wrestling, and Modern Grappling.* Toronto, ON: ECW Press, 2011.

Sharpe, J.P. "For Rent," advertisement. *Enterprise-Tocsin* (Indianola, MS), September 24, 1925.

Sheffer, Mary L. "Sullivan-Kilrain Fight." Mississippi Encyclopedia, June 13, 2022. https://mississippiencyclopedia.org.

Simpson County News (Mendenhall, MS). "IWF," advertisement. May 7, 1998.

Smith, Marquita. "Wrestlers Honor Slain Cab Driver." *Sun Herald* (Biloxi, MS), November 25, 1996.

Springer, Sylvia. "This Goliath Is Christian." *Express and News,* July 1, 1967.

Starr, Steve. Interview with author. Facebook Messenger, December 7, 2022. www.facebook.com.

Stone County Enterprise (Wiggins, MS). "Legion Boxing Show Draws Large Crowd." October 9, 1930.

———. "Legion to Sponsor Wrestling Here on Thursday, April 4." March 28, 1957.

———. "United Wrestling Federation," advertisement. August 10, 2000.

Sun Herald (Biloxi, MS). "Casino Magic," advertisement. February 18, 1994.

———. "Hurry, Get Your Tickets: Heart, Evita', Rasslin'." August 15, 1987.

———. "Tag Team Match Set for Legion Ring Wednesday." August 1,1955.

———. "World Class Championship Wrestling," advertisement. September 11, 1988.

———. "World Class Championship Wrestling," advertisement. February 17, 1989.

———. "Wrestling Returns to the Coast." December 14, 1994.

Sweeny, Sean "Fuller Family." Online World of Wrestling, April 28, 2014. www.onlineworldofwrestling.com.

———. "Uncle Elmer." Online World of Wrestling. April 28, 2014. www.onlineworldofwrestling.com.

Thomas, Bon. "8½ Footer Seeks Movie Career Over Side Show." *Casper (WY) Star-Tribune*, February 17, 1953.

Thrasher, Christopher David. *Fight Sports and American Masculinity: Salvation in Violence from 1607 to Present.* Jefferson, NC: McFarland & Company, 2015.

Times-Democrat (New Orleans, LA). "Wrestling Match To-Night." May 11, 1907.

Times Record News (Wichita Falls, TX), "Favorites Enter Mat Tournament." September 23, 1932.

Trench and Camp (Hattiesburg, MS). "Activities In and About the 'Y' Buildings at Camp Shelby." October 24, 1917.

———. "Athletic Notes." December 25, 1917.

———. "No. 4 Not Keen for Matless Wrestle Gladiators." January 7, 1918.

———. "Star Wrestlers Hold Thanksgiving Day Bouts." December 10, 1917.

———. "Wrestlers and Boxers Fill Bill at K. of C. Hall." April 14, 1918.

Turner, Mack. "Curtis Gets Draw with Reynolds in Wrestling Match." *Wichita Falls (TX) Times*, December 10, 1932.

United States Census Bureau. "1930 United States Census." Familysearch.org.

———. "1940 United States Federal Census." Ancestry Library. www.ancestrylibrary.com.

———. "1950 United States Federal Census." Ancestry Library. www.ancestrylibrary.com.

United States Department of Justice. Immigration and Naturalization Service. Petition for Naturalization, 620, Washington, D.C., GPO. Ancestry Library. www.ancestrylibrary.com.

Upton, Dennis. Interview with author, October 22, 2022.

Van Vliet, Chris. "Marko Stunt on his Size, Signing with AEW, Luchasarus, Jungle Boy, Dynamite." YouTube, October 9, 2019. https://youtu.be/jbSFrmKuivQ.

Vicksburg (MS) Evening Post. "Local Wrestler Awarded a Draw." March 13, 1917.

———. "Program Complete for Convention of American Legion." August 9, 1920.

———. "Wrestling Match Here Next Week." May 11, 1911.

———. "Wrestling Matches End in Near Fight." March 17, 1917.

Watts, "Cowboy" Bill, and Scott Williams. *The Cowboy and the Cross: The Bill Watts Story: Rebellion, Wrestling, and Redemption.* Toronto, ON: ECW Press, 2006, p. 132.

Webster Progress (Eupora, MS). "Eupora Lions Will Sponsor Wrestling Match." May 11, 1967.

Weekly Democrat-Times (Greenville, MS). "Benefit Athletic Exhibition." January 3, 1903.

Weekly Democrat (Natchez, MS). "Wrestling and Boxing," advertisement. January 15, 1930.

W.E. Pegues Funeral Directors. "Bob Arnold," obituary. April 13, 2022. https://www.legacy.com.

Wetherbee, Don. "Delta All Sports." *Delta Democrat-Times* (Greenville, MS), February 1, 1938.

Wheatley, Joseph. "Meet Jim Londos, the Highest Drawing Star in Wrestling History That No One Has Heard Of." The Sportster, February 1, 2022. https://www.thesportster.com.

Wheeler, Jimmy, ed. "Billy Romanoff." *Professional Wrestling Historical Society.* December 7, 2019. https://www.prowrestlinghistoricalsociety.com.

White, Connie. "Tallest Man Returns for Visit in Area." *Clarksdale (MS) Press Register*, October 2, 1981.

Whitlock, Dustin. "Mississippi Wrestlers Debuts on TNT." *Scott County Times* (Forest, MS), October 23, 2019.

Winona (MS) Times. "Dixie AllStar Professional Wrestling," advertisement. September 29, 1983.

———. "Jack Dempsey." November 7, 1930.

Winston County Journal (Louisville, MS). "AWF Championship Wrestling," advertisement. February 24, 1984.

———. "Central Wrestling Federation," advertisement. August 25, 1993.

———. "D.W.A. Professional Wrestling," advertisement. April 2, 1982.

———. "Mid South All Star Production Pro Wrestling," advertisement. August 23, 1973.

———. "Professional Wrestling Is Announced." March 7, 1968.

———. "Wrestling Returns." June 10, 1987.

Wrestling Data. www.wrestlingdata.com. 2001–23.

Wrestling New Center Contributors. *Wrestling News Center Blog.* 2008–23. https://www.wrestlingnewscenter.com.

Wrestling Titles. 1995–2013. https://www.wrestling-titles.com.

Yazoo Herald (Yazoo City, MS). "Fighters Draw Here Thursday." September 10, 1926.

———. "Star Wrestlers to Appear Monday." February 17, 1939.

———. "Wrestlers to Show Here Next Thursday Night at Ideal Theatre Building." April 23, 1926.

ABOUT THE AUTHOR

J effrey Martin lives in Fulton, Mississippi, with his wife, Sarah, and two children, Silas and Jude. He has been a public librarian for twelve years. This is his first book. He was inspired to write this book by Silas, who has become a wrestling superfan in recent years. It reminded Martin of his own love and devotion for the sport as a young man.

Visit us at
www.historypress.com

Printed in the USA
CPSIA information can be obtained
at www.ICGtesting.com
LVHW010009080224
771084LV00003B/124